David Carter
American Revolutionary War Soldier, his Family and Their Descendants

David Carter
American Revolutionary War Soldier, his Family and Their Descendants

compiled by

Robert D. McCloud

Genealogy Publishing Group
Amherst, Massachusetts

Published 2021 by Genealogy Publishing Group, a division of White River Press
PO Box 3561, Amherst, MA 01004 • genealogypublishinggroup.com

ISBN: 978-1-935052-81-4

Cover Design by Lufkin Graphic Designs
Norwich, Vermont • www.LufkinGraphics.com

Library of Congress Cataloging-in-Publication Data

Names: McCloud, Robert D. (Robert Davis), 1938- compiler.
Title: David Carter, American revolutionary soldier, his family and their
   descendants / compiled by Robert Davis McCloud.
Description: Amherst, Massachusetts : Genealogy Publishing Group, 2021. |
   Includes bibliographical references and index. | Summary: "A genealogy
   of the life of David Carter, American Revolutionary soldier, his family
   and their descendants. With photos, charts, index"-- Provided by
   publisher.
Identifiers: LCCN 2021062355 | ISBN 9781935052814 (hardcover)
Subjects: LCSH: Carter, David, Sr., 1758-1850. | Carter family. |
   Georgia--Genealogy.
Classification: LCC CS71.C323 2021 | DDC 929/.20973--dc23/eng/20220103
LC record available at https://lccn.loc.gov/2021062355

Contents

Part I

Part II

Part III

Acknowledgements

The story of the life of David Carter Sr. has been greatly expanded by the information contained in two original documents and one independent compilation of Carter family information. David Carter Sr. applied for Revolutionary War pension benefits on two different occasions. The earlier application was submitted in 1823 at the court of Pendleton District, South Carolina, while the second was submitted in 1832 at court in Franklin County, Georgia. Pendleton District, SC and Franklin County, GA are separated by the width of the Savannah River, which serves as their boundary.

The information contained in both petitions is virtually the same, which speaks well of David Carter's state of mind during the time frame of both petitions. This fact comforts us of a certain amount of accuracy to his statements.

The third source of information and from an independent compilation was found in the 1933 publication entitled *History of Hart County(GA),* written by John William Baker. Considering the time frame at which this material was compiled, the result is excellent, especially information concerning later family members.

Various researchers have tried, over the years, to connect David Carter Sr. to the Carters of Green County, TN. This suspected familial link was encouraged when it was discovered Daniel Carter of Green County, TN signed an affidavit for David Carter's 1823 Revolutionary War pension petition. Daniel Carter stated he knew "the circumstances of David's Family and his service to the Revolution well." This Daniel Carter is believed to same Daniel Carter who married Nancy Cobb on February 22, 1782, in Wilkes County, NC. This marriage took place nearly at the same time David Carter, Sr. married Mahitable Cobb, which is also believed to have taken place in Wilkes County, NC. While certain circumstances suggest a family relationship, there is no documented proof of their familial ties.

David and Mehitable Cobb Carter's descendants have shown the same sense of adventure and steely determination to blaze new paths in the conquest of what has become the United States of America as their ancestors had. They have crossed the great plains in covered wagons, some have viewed the mighty Pacific, while others have come back to where it all started. They have served in the new nation's wars serving with honor and are examples of what good useful citizens to this nation should be.

This book would not be possible without the assistance of my daughter Cheryl McCloud Helm in getting this book published. Proudly this is something she has done many times before with the publishing of my five genealogy works.

Dedication

The book is dedication to the memory of Sherwood Johnson Carter and Margaret Nancy Speir Carter. Sherwood, probably better known to family and friends by his nickname Nick, was the determined collector of most of the material in this collection compiling many notebooks along the way.

Nick and Nancy became the parents of four lively children, Sherwood Jr., Donald, Richard and Debra. Nancy, a gifted artist, had a wonderful knack of telling colorful stories of her Red River County, Texas childhood. Nick served in the U. S. Army seeing service in three wars, World War II, Korea and Viet Nam.

PART I

David Carter Sr.

David Carter Sr. was born February 20, 1758, in East New Jersey. At a young age David with his family moved to the Virginia frontier where David grew to adulthood. The exact date of this move is unknown but with an appreciation of the unfolding historical events on the frontier, a time frame of this move can be created with a small amount of speculation.

The French and Indian War started in 1756 pitting the French and their Indian allies against the British and their colonial allies. The French and Indian War ended on the Virginia frontier with the Treaty of Paris about 1763. In the spring of 1763, settlers and land speculators started moving in large numbers onto the frontier. The numbers were so large the British were forced to issue the Proclamation of 1763, which prohibited colonials from moving beyond the slopes of the Allegheny Mountains. This proclamation, however, did little to stop the migration of settlers.

In 1768, the Treaty of Fort Stanwix was signed that allowed all the lands south and east of the Ohio River to pass under British control. This treaty gave even greater impetus to the settlers to move to the frontier. The problem with this treaty was that the Iroquois Nation who signed the treaty was only one of many Indian tribes who used the same land. This, of course, caused great conflict between the settlers and the Indian tribes who did not sign the treaty.

It was during this period of vast movement by settlers to the frontier and the ever-expanding discontent of the various Indian tribes that David Carter and his family moved to the Virginia frontier. The time frame for the move had to be between 1763 and 1768.

It is known with certainty that the Carter family was in place at the Virginia frontier in 1774 because that was when David Carter, who was only sixteen years old, first entered service of the Virginia Colony. He was then living on the Monongahela River. David volunteered entering the service in the fall of 1774 at Redstone, Virginia under the command of Capt. Owens guarding the frontier against the Shawnee Indians. He was stationed at the home of Capt. Owens on the Monongahela. During this same time, a major defeat of the Indians took place at the Battle of Point Pleasant on October 10, 1774, that virtually ended the so-called Lord Dunmore's War. An uneasy peace along the frontier settled for the winter over the snowy caps of the western mountains of Virginia.

David saw service again in June 1775, this time he was drafted. Following this service, David Carter and probably with other members of his family; moved to Surry County, North Carolina, arriving there in 1777. In 1778, Surry County was divided into Surry County and Wilkes County. The precise county David Carter lived in is uncertain as the names of the two counties appear to be used often almost interchangeably in the written records of the time.

In the spring of 1778, David entered as a volunteer for the Militia of North Carolina, serving under the command of Capt. Martin and Major Lewis as a rifleman in Benjamin Cleveland's Regiment. David served four months at this time and was mainly sent out in search for Tories.

1

He was involved in several skirmishes, especially one located at "the Shallow Ford on the Yadkin River, Bryant's Settlement."

In June 1779, David entered the service of the main army under Gen. Griffith Rutherford at Pee Dee below Salisbury. On August 7, 1780, Gen. Rutherford's army eventually joined the command of Gen. Horatio Gates after which they marched out to meet the British at Camden, South Carolina. Here the Americans were severely defeated on August15-16, 1780. David Carter and Gen. Rutherford were captured, with David being confined to prison ships in Charleston harbor.

An American doctor, Dr. Fayssoux, who treated the prisoners, wrote what he witnessed, "that these men were confined on board prison ships, in numbers by no means proportional to the size of the vessel, immediately after a march of one hundred and twenty miles, in the most sickly season of this unhealthy climate." These vessels were generally infected with small pox. The British did, eventually, allow inoculation of prisoners, but that did little to offset the putrid dysentery that repeatedly affected the prisoners. David Carter served 11 months aboard three ships, The Concord, the King George and the Fidelity. He was exchanged at Jamestown, Virginia in August 1781.

A family story states that during his imprisonment David was involved in an attempt to capture the ship where he was imprisoned. "The plan was for them to rush the prison guards and overpower them. David was selected to lead the assault. At the given signal he did so, but was not supported by the other prisoners. Several of the guards grappled with him and after administering a sever mauling, threw him down the hatch among the other prisoners." This story was found in an article that appeared in *The Hartwell Sun*, Hartwell, GA on July 7, 1902, written by the Honorable James M. Carter, a grandson of David Carter Sr.

After David was exchanged at Jamestown, VA, he found himself "near 500 miles from home without money or clothing, and compelled to beg and live on charity." He was hampered so severely by sickness and hardship, "that he was unable to travel more than about ten miles a day." At this rate of travel it would have taken him nearly a month and a half to reach his home in North Carolina.

However, it appears it did not take David long to regain his health because he enlisted in the militia again on November 11, 1781, serving as a substitute under Capt. Johnson. He was marched by Capt. Johnson and Col. Isaacs to Randolph County in search of Col. Fanning and Tories. His service this time lasted three months. This was the end of David Carter's participation in the American Revolutionary War struggle.

David Carter married Mahitable Cobb, probably in Wilkes County, North Carolina sometime about the year 1786. Mahitable Cobb's family is unknown. It appears the Carter family moved to Pendleton District, South Carolina about the year 1787. The Cherokee Indians had ceded this area to the state of South Carolina by the Treaty of Hopewell on November 25, 1785. The new district had been part of the old Ninety-Six District. The divisions of local government in South Carolina, at this time, were called districts instead of counties. It appears many families from Wilkes County, North Carolina relocated to Pendleton District at this time. This also included

David's old commander, Col. Benjamin Cleveland, who also moved to Pendleton District becoming a famous, it not notorious, judge there.

Pension Application of David Carter S16335
Transcribed and annotated by C. Leon Harris

State of Georgia   } S.S.
County of Franklin |

On this eleventh day of October in the year Eighteen Hundred and thirty two personally appeared before the Superior Court for the County & State aforesaid now sitting David Carter a resident of Capt. Royston's District in the County and state aforesaid aged Seventy three years, who being first duly sworn according to Law doth on his oath make the following Declaration in order to obtain the Benefit of the Act of Congress passed June 7 1832. That he entered the service of the United States in the Militia of the State of North Carolina as a volunteer in Surrey [sic: Surry] County under Capt Martin in the Spring of 1778 was kept out scouting after the Tories under Capt Martin & Major Lewis and served four months in this kind of duty

And again entered the main army of General [Griffith] Rutherford at Peedee [sic: Pee Dee River], below Salisbury North Carolina in June 1779 and was under Capt Bostwick [sic: Absalom Bostick] in the Company and after being about a month under him was shifted to a rifle Company (does not recollect the Captains name as the Capt & Lieut both went home a few days afterwards) was marched under Rutherford to Camden South Carolina, & was in the Battle there under Gen'l. Gates [Horatio Gates, 16 Aug 1780], and the army was defeated at Camden and deponent was taken prisoner & carried to Charleston S.C. & was detained at Charleston & in the Prison ships eleven months & four days, & was then carried to Jamestown Virginia, where he was exchanged in August 1781, altogether he was a prisoner as before stated Eleven months and four days. After being exchanged as aforesaid he returned home after a service of Fifteen months in this last campaign

And in Wilkes County North Carolina, and about 1st November 1781, he again entered the army under Capt. Johnson as a substitute (does not recollect the name of the person for whom he substituted) was marched by Capt. Johnson & Col [Elijah] Isaacs down to Randolph County & to other places after Col. Fannig [sic: David Fanning] and other Tories & had several skirmishes with the Tories, was out in this Service three months & was dismissed by Capt Johnson

In addition to the above & before said service He entered the service in Redstone in Virginia, under Capt Owens, and was sent to guard the frontier against the Shawnee Indians, was stationed at Capt Owens house on Monongehela river [sic: Monongahela River, probably in present Monongalia County WV]; Served three months & was discharged by Capt Owens And again entered for one month & served against said Indians under Lieutenant Lewis at Dunkards station. this service was in the fall of year 1774. that is the first three months, the last month was in June 1775.

Served altogether Two years and two months as aforesaid

1. Was born in East New Jersey in the year 1758 left there with his parents when very young & was raised in Virginia.

2. Does not know whether there is any record of his age.

3. When first called into service he lived on Monongahela on the frontier of Virginia, from there he removed to North Carolina Surrey County in 1777. Since the war he has lived in Pendleton District South Carolina until the fall of 1825 when he removed to his present residence & has remained there ever since

4. Served as a volunteer, except three months he was a substitute & the last month he served in Virginia he was drafted.

5 Recollects Genl. Gates, Genl Smallwood [William Smallwood of MD] & Genl De Kalb who was killed at Camden

6 Received several Discharges but they are lost, one from Capt Owens one from Capt Bostwick & one from Capt Johnson. does not recollect others

7. is known to Henry Parks of the County first aforesaid who saw him in service after the Tories. is also known to Wilbur A. McMillin and to Samuel Hymer a preacher of the Gospel who resides in his neighborhood & who can all testify to his character for veracity & to their belief of his

3

having been a Soldier of the Revolution

He hereby relinquishes every claim whatever to a pension or annuity except the present and declares that his name is not on the pension roll of the agency of any State, only that he now receives a pension of Sixty Dollars from the State of South Carolina, under a similar statement to the above.   David hisXmark Carter

State of Georgia   } SS
County of Franklin }
          On this 22ⁿᵈ day of July in the year eighteen Hundred and thirty three, personally appeared before me, Benjamin Stonecypher an acting Justice of the Peace in and for said County David Carter who has heretofore subscribed and sworn to the original Declaration to which this is attached and who being again duly Sworn on oath saith That by reason of old age, and the consequent loss of memory he cannot swear positively as to the precise length of his services. But according to the best of his recollection he served not less than the periods mentioned below, and in the following grades, viz

For four months in 1778 he served as a private under Capt Martin & Col. Cleveland

For three months in 1780 he served as private partly under Capt Bostwick partly rifle Co. was
          under Gen. Rutherford, does not recollect the Colonel's name

For Eleven months and 4 days from August 1780 till August 1781 he was a prisoner to the
          British & was kept in the Prison ships "Concord," "King George" and "Fidelity" at
          Charleston, he served this time as a private.

For one month in Nov'r 1781 he served as a private under Capt Johnson & Col Isaacs

For two months in Dec'r 1781 & Jan'y 1782 he served under Capt Beverly & Col Isaacs as a
          private horseman.

For three month in 1774 he served as a private under Capt Owens & Col Morgan   }
For one month in 1775 he served as a private under Lieut Lewis & Col Morgan   }
                    This service was against the Shawanee Indians   }

Served altogether for fourteen months as a private, and Eleven months as a prisoner of War he served with an embodied Corps called into service by competent authority, that he was during the time either in the field or in Garrison, and for the time during which the service was performed he was not employed in any civil pursuit, and for such service he claims a pension. He has understood that his pension in South Carolina is discontinued by some late Act. He knows of no person now in life whose testimony he is able to procure to prove his Services, other than the proof attached to his original Declaration, to which he refers for particular of Service   David hisXmark Carter

David Carter, Sr.'s Southern Campaign American Revolution Pension Application

Tombstone of David Carter, Sr.

The Kershaw – Cornwallis House, Camden, South Carolina

The area around Pendleton District, SC had deposits of coal and iron ore and several iron mills were established there. David Carter was involved in one of these mills. On March 23, 1793, David and Robert Gabie of Lincoln County, NC each purchased from John Grissam one-third rights of an iron works that also included a grist mill. Five Pounds Sterling was the price each man paid for his share. The mill was located on Twenty-Six Mile Creek. The witnesses to the transaction were Lewis Cobb (probable kinsman to David's wife) and James Anderson. David and Robert sold their interest in the mill operation to Samuel Tate on March 2, 1795. Samuel paid them each Five Pounds Sterling for the property, the price they had originally paid. When David sold this property to Tate, his wife Mahitable Cobb Carter had to give a deposition of agreement to the sale, which she did.

David Carter sold additional land on March 28, 1808, to David Sloan. He sold forty acres for Sixty dollars but the location of this land was not given, nor when he had acquired the land. One curious but interesting item in the deed stated that one John McMillon, Esquire, was noted as living on this land.

On June 17, 1813, David Carter purchased 274 acres of land from Benjamin C. Yancey for $428.00. This land had been surveyed by Lewis David Yancey on July 12, 1786, and was located on a branch of Twenty-Three Mile Creek, on the waters of the Keowa River. A portion of this 274 acres tract had already been sold to Archibald McElroy. The deed for this property was not recorded at the courthouse until January 19, 1815.

Veronika A. Jackson and Uncle Sherwood Carter, Jr.
Revolutionary War Re-Enactors

David Carter sold this land to his son Micajah Carter on April 22, 1815, for $400.00. Micajah Carter then in turn sold this property to his brother David Carter Jr. on August 14, 1817, who paid the same price his brother had paid for the property, $400.00. Witnesses to the transaction were John Acre and Joseph Carter. Who this Joseph Carter was is unknown.

David Carter Jr. sold this property to Archibald McElroy on November 27, 1820. This was the same Archibald McElroy who had been involved in the original sale of the property. One of the property lines mentioned in the deed records was that of Abeal Carter's property. Who this Abeal Carter was is also unknown.

David Carter Sr. was found listed on the 1820 Pendleton district census. Micajah Carter and David Carter Jr. were not found on these documents; which presumes they had already moved to Georgia by this date. On November 10, 1823, David Carter (Sr.) appeared in court and made a petition to the State of South Carolina for an "Annuity" or other relief relative to his situation, which he described in this fashion. "your petitioner begs leave to state that he is now in the sixth-fifth year of his age- that he has a wife about 63 years of age. That by misfortune your petitioner has lost all his property and is unable now to labour sufficiently to make a comfortable support for himself and wife." At this time David Carter (Sr.) stated he had been living in Pendleton District for thirty-three years.

Shortly after receiving his yearly pension of $60.00 from the state of South Carolina, David and the remaining members of his family moved to rejoin his sons Micajah and David Carter Jr. in Franklin County, Georgia. The move was not really that far, just across the Savannah River from where he formerly lived in South Carolina. This was in the fall of 1825. He settled on property near the mouth of Lightwood Log Creek, where it empties into the Savannah River. Lightwood Log Creek was the county line between Wilkes and Franklin Counties when Elbert County was created from part of Wilkes, it then became the county line between Elbert and Franklin Counties. In 1854, when Hart County was created from parts of Elbert and Franklin, Lightwood Log Creek was no longer on the county line but was completely in Hart County.

David Carter Sr. appeared at the Superior Court of Franklin County, Georgia on October 11, 1832, where he applied for a pension due him because of his service in the Revolutionary War. This pension was in response to an Act of Congress that was passed on June 7, 1832, to benefit veterans. This deposition contains much of the same material covered in his 1823 petition in South Carolina. A copy of David's 1832 pension application is seen on pages 3 and 4.

The tombstone over David Carter's grave in Hart County, GA has a date of death as December 16, 1949. However, this date is in doubt as David Carter, age 96, was found within the home of his son Micajah Carter for the 1850 Franklin County, GA census. This combined with the 1902 statement by the Hon. James M. Carter, son of Micajah Carter, who said in a local newspaper article that, " I knew him (his grandfather) for 20 years. He died in 1850, and was buried at Mt. Zion Church, Hart County.

All the graves at Mt. Zion Methodist Church were removed to New Harmony Methodist Church starting in May through September 1961 because of the creation of a dam on the Savannah River in effect creating Lake Hartwell. It is believed by certain family members that several of the stones over the Carter graves were left and are now under water. More information about the re-interment may be found under the web site Lake Hartwell Cemetery/ Grave Re-interment, Corps of Engineers, Hartwell, GA.

*Carter Family Graves at Mt. Zion Methodist Church that were
removed to New Harmony Methodist Church dated 1961*

David Carter Sr. and Mahitable Cobb Carter were the parents of three known children.

1. Micajah Carter
2. David Carter Jr.
3. Mahitable Carter

Micajah Carter

Micajah Carter was born probably in Wilkes County, North Carolina about 1787, the son of David Carter Sr. and Mahitable Cobb Carter. He moved with his family to Pendleton district, SC, at about 1790. The use of the word "County" did not come into use in South Carolina until after the Civil War.

It is believed that Micajah Carter served in the War of 1812. A statement found in J.W. Baker's *History of Hart County* makes these comments, "Micajah Carter was a soldier in the War of 1812, and while we have no record that his brother, David Carter, Jr. was a soldier in said war, it is a well-authenticated tradition that he also served in the War of 1812 along with his brother, Micajah." There is a record of Micajah Carter serving in the War of 1812. He served as a private in Austin's Regt., South Carolina Militia.

Micajah Carter married the relict of Isaac J. Barrett, Nancy Goolsby Barrett, sometime before 1818, probably in Pendleton district, SC. Nancy was the widow of Isaac J. Barrett, the daughter of William Goolsby.

Micajah Carter was not found on either the South Carolina or Georgia census for the 1820. Yet, he appears to have been already residing in Georgia because on October 14, 1820, Micajah Carter signed a quit claim registered in Pendleton District, South Carolina over to John Haynie Jr. This release was on a claim of land deeded to the heirs of Stephen Haynie by John Haynie Sr. The importance of the claim lies in the fact that it was deeded while Micajah Carter was living in Franklin County, GA. So, he was in Georgia by late 1820, but appears to have been simply missed by the census takers. He was found for the 1830 and 1840 census living in Franklin County, GA.

Nancy Goolsby Barrett Carter died at a date unknown. Micajah Carter married for the second time to Mrs. Mourning Earp on January 22, 1850, in Elbert County, GA. The Micajah Carter family was found for the 1850 Georgia census living in Franklin County. The 63 year old farmer, Micajah Carter, was listed with his 58 year old wife, Mourning Carter. Also in the family enumeration were Micajah's sister Mahitable Carter, age 48 and his father David Carter, age 96.

Hart County was created in 1853 out of portions of Franklin and Elbert Counties. The county was named for an American Revolutionary War heroin Nancy Hart, who fought against Tories. In an election held in February, 1853, Micajah Carter was elected on of the five sitting Inferior Court Justices. The Lightwood Log Creek community where the Carters lived was now located entirely within the new county.

James M. Carter, on January 27, 1857, sold 57 acres of land situated on "little lightwood log creek" to Micajah Carter for $850.00. The land was described as "being the tract of land where James M. Carter now lives." One boundary of this tract mentioned David Carter's property lying to the east of this property. This James M. Carter was the nephew of Micajah Carter, not his son who was also named James M. Carter.

The 1860 Georgia, Hart County census shows Micajah Carter, age 72, and Morning (sic) Carter, age 68, living in Dooley's District. Within this family listing was a 28 year old William B. Carter, who was a lawyer. This young man, who was born in Georgia, appears to be Micajah's nephew William Balus Carter, the son of David Carter Jr. William B. Carter died in the Civil War in 1865.

Micajah Carter and Mourning Carter were again located in Dooley's District for the 1870 Georgia census. He was 83 year old retired farmer, while she was 80. At that time Micajah declared $4,000.00 worth of real estate property value and $1,000.00 worth of personal property. This was certainly a good estate for the times, this was also the last census for Micajah Carter.

A few lines down on the same census page was the family of Anderson Sanders, a farmer, and his wife Caroline and their four young children. Also recorded in the home was Lavina Carter, age 73 and retired. Mrs. Carter relationship to this family is not clear.

Micajah Carter died on March 25, 1876, he was buried at Mt. Zion Methodist Church where he had been a long-time member. His funeral was preached by a friend of fifty-five years, the Rev. Henry Tyler. The Rev. W. T. Norman also assisted in the funeral. Micajah Carter was buried

Mount Zion Methodist cemetery where many of his family were also buried. This cemetery was eventually moved in 1961 to New Hope Methodist cemetery.

The will of Micajah Carter mentions a daughter Malissa. In item "Fifth - I give and bequeath unto my son-in-law, E. W. Roebuck, in trust for my daughter Malissa C. Roebuck, four hundred dollars to be paid out of money arising for the sale of my property."

There were also provisions in the will for his wife, Mourning. However, she died a few months later on August 5, 1876. She was buried beside her former husband at Ruhamah Methodist Church, Anderson County, SC.

Micajah Carter was the parent of two known children.

1. James M. Carter
2. Malissa Carter, nee wife of E. W. Roebuck

James Monroe Carter

James M. Carter was born in what was then Franklin County, GA on February 11, 1822, the son of Micajah Carter and Nancy Goolsby Barrett Carter. The area where James was born later became Hart County. James's name has also come to us as James Monroe Carter. The Find a Grave index records the father of Florence M. Carter as James Munroe Carter.

The place where James M. Carter was born was about a half-mile from the Savannah River and one hundred yards from Lightwood Creek. The creek was at that time the dividing line between Elbert County and Franklin County and served as one of the important watercourses for trade in the area.

For twelve years James M. Carter ran a boat on the Savannah River. The boat was a flat bottom boat that was pushed along with long poles. This was how freight was moved to Augusta, GA, then one of the chief cities in the state. The trip down river required about three days while the trip up river required about seven days. The boats carried cotton, flour or corn down river while the return trip carried dry goods, coffee, sugar, salt and iron. "Western corn, flour and meat were unknown in this area."

In 1846, James M. Carter married Mary Louisa Clark of Abbeville, SC. She was the daughter of Mary Alston Clark who was a first cousin of Governor Alston, who married Theodosia Burr, the daughter of Aaron Burr. She was related to five governors in their area, probably South Carolina.

The 1860 Georgia, Elbert County census locates this family with an Elberton address. James was a farmer with $10,000 worth of real estate value and $11, 235 of personal property. There were four children in the home at that time, A. E. Carter (f), age 12, J. F. M. Carter (m), age 8, Georgia Carter (f), age 5 and L.C Carter (m) age 1. Mr. Carter owned a large portion of land in Elbert County. He served as Senator for Elbert County in 1859-1860.

James M. Carter served as an Orderly Sergeant in Company 'H' of Carswell's Brigade during the Civil War. His last service was officer in charge of the Pontoon Corps that brought pontoon boats from Augusta to Petersburg Ferry on the Savannah River. He brought the pontoons that enabled President Jefferson Davis to cross the river on his way to Washington, GA.

The 1870 Georgia, Elbert County census locates the Carter family still living at an Elberton address. James was a 47 year old farmer, his wife Mary L. was a 40 year old housewife. There were seven children in the home at that time, Amea L. Carter, age 20, Florence M. Carter (m), age 17, George E. Carter, age 12, William Y. Carter, age 8, Katie Carter, age 7, James N. Carter, age 5, Leolla A. Carter, age 3.

The 1880 Georgia, Elbert County census finds this family with James and Louisa at home with three of their children still at home, Katie, age 17, James, age 16 and Leola, age 12. The enumerator or recorder for the census was James M. Carter.

The 1900 Hart County census, Alford area, locates James M. Carter Sr. living within the home of his son James M. Carter Jr. He was 79 years old.

The Honorable James M. Carter died on May 16, 1908, at the residence of his son-in-law, the Rev. T. A. Thornton, Hartwell, GA. He was carried by railway to Elberton where he was laid to rest in the city cemetery. The funeral services were conducted by Dr. J. H. Mashburn, presiding Elder of Elberton District, and the Rev. J. H. Wall, a lifelong friend.

John William Baker in his book *History of Hart County* concluded his biography of James M. Carter with the statement that the descendants of David Carter Sr. were patriotic and readily responded to their country's call. Citing the history of "James M. Carter, grandson of David Sr., served as a soldier in the War Between the States; W. Y. Carter and F. M. Carter, sons of James M., served in the Spanish-American War, W. Y. as Captain and F. M. as Quartermaster; Y. Cade Carter, son of F. M. served in the same war as Sergeant; Preston B. Carter, son of James Carter Jr., and grandson of James M. Carter, served in the World War and was killed in action overseas."

James M. Carter and Mary Louisa Clark Carter were the parents of seven known children. The listing recorded below is from Baker's book *History of Hart County.*

1. Mrs. McAlpin Arnold of Elberton
2. Mrs. T. A. Thornton of Hartwell
3. Capt. Florence Micajah Carter of Hartwell
4. Capt. William Yancey Carter of Hartwell
5. James Monroe Carter Jr. of Hart County, GA
6. Mrs. H. C. Mickel of Elberton
7. Mrs. Kate Grubb of Texas

Florence Micajah Carter

Florence M. Carter was born August 7, 1853, the son of James M. Carter and Mary Louisa Clark Carter. Florence married Julia Eleanor Speed of Lowndesville, Abbeville County, SC. She was born in 1841, the daughter of E. P. Speed and Eleanor J. Baker.

Florence M. Carter and his son Y. Cade Carter joined with Florence's brother William Y. Carter to serve together in the Spanish-American War in 1898. Florence joined as a private, but quickly became a sergeant in Company 'E,' 3 U. S. Volunteer Infantry.

At one time, Florence M. Carter served as Town Marshall for Hartwell and was in charge of collecting the "street tax" which was $3.00 per year. This tax was used to do work on the streets in the town. If one could not pay the tax, work was accepted in place of the tax.

The 1900 Georgia, Hart County census locates the Carter family living in Hartwell Town. Florence was working as a 'policeman', he was 46 years old and married for 25 years. He was the parent of seven children with six still living and four still in the home at this listing, Cade, Annie Lizzie, Alston and Louise.

Eleanor Speed Carter died April 10, 1932, in Anderson, SC. Florence M. Carter died October 14, 1932, in Anderson, Anderson County, South Carolina. He was a 79-year-old widower, his occupation was given as 'retired officer'. The 'Find a Grave Index' records Florence Carter's wife as Julia Eleanor Carter. His father was given as James Munroe Carter, his mother as Louisa Carter.

Florence and Eleanor Speed Carter are buried in Silver Brook Cemetery in Anderson, SC. They were the parents of five known children.

1. William Pickens Carter
2. Yancy Cade Carter, born Nov. 1877
3. Annie Lizzie Carter, born March 1883
4. Alston (Buddy) Carter, born Dec, 1884
5. Mrs. Louise Carter Payne, born July 1887

William Pickens Carter

William Pickens Carter was born 1876, the son of Florence M. Carter and Eleanor Speed Carter. William married Effie Henry Satterfield, she was the daughter of William Henry and Martha Eleanor Page Satterfield.

William Pickens Carter was a railroad mechanic who was scalded to death in the Atlanta roundhouse at the age of 33. The exact date and particulars of the death have yet to be discovered. What is known is that for the 1900 Hart County census, Hartwell town, Effie Carter and her son Cary Carter were living in the home of her widowed mother Martha Satterfield. Effie had been married 4 years which would give her a marriage date of 1896, the census record stated she was the mother of one child.

Effie Carter married L.A. O'Neal on June 24, 1909, in Hart County, GA. He was engineer in charge of construction of the Calabra Cut in the Panama Canal. The 1910 Hart County census, Town District discovers Cary Carter living within the home of his grandmother Martha Satterfield, he was 10 years old. His mother had started a family with Mr. O'Neal.

Carey Cade Carter registered for the draft on September 12, 1918. He was working as an auto mechanic at Madison Machine and Auto Company in Madison Morgan, GA. Carey was described as tall, medium build, blue eyes with light brown hair. Carey's mother Mrs. L.A. O'Neal signed the registration card for her son.

The O'Neal family was found for the 1920 Hart County, Town District listing Effie and her husband Lucius O' Neal listing their three children Cristine, John, and Timothy. O'Neal's occupation was given as a "Proprietor of a garage"

Effie Satterfield and Lucius O'Neal were the parents of five known children; Cristine O'Neal, John Henry O'Neal, Michael O'Neal, Tim O'Neal and Ralph O'Neal.

Effie Satterfield and William Pickens Carter was the parent of one child.

1. Carey Cade Carter

Carey Cade Carter

Carey Cade Carter was born May 3, 1898, the son of William Pickens Carter and Effie Satterfield. Carey married Nina Brown Teasley, the daughter of Oscar A. Teasley and Nancy Lee Brown Teasley.

Nina Teasley was first married to William Franklin Pittard Jr. and they had one child William Franklin Pittard III.

Carey Cade Carter died October 29, 1951. Nina Teasley Carter later married James F. Wilson with no issue.

Children;

1. Carey Cade Carter Jr.
2. Nina Teasley Carter
3. William Oscar Carter
4. Martha Eleanor Carter, deceased
5. Florence Louisa Carter

Carey Cade Carter Jr.

Carey Cade Carter Jr. was born December 11, 1919, the son of Carey Cade Carter Sr. and Nina Brown Teasley Carter. Carey Cade Carter Jr. married Louise Cribbs of Anderson, SC.

Children;

1. Carey Cade Carter III
2. Martha Eleanor Carter
3. Allen Wilcox Carter

William Oscar Carter

William Oscar Carter was born July 11, 1923, the son of Carey Cade Carter Sr. William married Helen Joan Harris on February 11, 1942. She was born in Kentucky, the daughter of James H. and Lottie Harris. William and Helen were the parents of one child, they were later divorced.

William later married Mary Helen Brooks on June 30, 1954. Her parents were James Addison and Lola Smith Brooks.

William O. Carter is an attorney practicing in Hartwell, GA. He is the parent of five children with two wives.

1. Robert Harris Carter
2. James William Carter
3. Richard Brooks Carter
4. Stephen Clay Carter
5. Mary Brooks Carter

James William Carter

James William Carter was born May 5, 1955, the son of William Oscar Carter and Mary Helen Brooks Carter.

James is a graduate of the Medical College of Georgia. James married Cynthia Ann Hudgens, the daughter of Harvey Lee and Reba Coile Hudgens. There are two children of this family.

1. Meredith Ann Carter
2. James William Carter Jr.

Richard Brooks Carter

Richard Brooks Carter was born January 26, 1956, the son of William Oscar Carter and Mary Helen Brooks Carter. Richard married Melissa _____, with one child born to this couple. They later divorced. He lives with his son in Nashville, TN.

1. Richard Brooks Carter Jr.

Stephen Clay Carter

Stephen Clay Carter was born May 30, 1958, the son of William Oscar Carter and Mary Helen Brooks Carter. He practices law with his father in Hartwell, GA. Stephen married Kathlyn Hamby in December 1991. There are two children of this family.

1. Kathlyn Elizabeth Carter
2. Emily Brooks Carter

Mary Brooks Carter

Mary Brooks Carter was born _____, the daughter of William Oscar Carter and Mary Helen Brooks Carter. She married William Paul Hogan in 1990. Both are employed in management positions in Hartwell and Anderson. There are two children of this family.

1. William Paul Hogan Jr.
2. Carter Westin Hogan

Yancy Cade Carter

Yancy Cade Carter was born November 12, 1877, the son of Florence Carter and Eleanor Speed. Yancy Cade Carter married Nelle Beasley Carter. Yancy Cade Carter joined with his father and his uncle William Yancey Carter to serve in the Spanish-American War. Joining as a private he quickly rose to sergeant in Company 'E', 3 U.S. Volunteer Infantry.

The family was located on the 1940 South Carolina, Abbeville, Lowndesville census, Yancy C. Carter was 62 years old working as 'cotton weigher' at a cotton warehouse. His wife Nelle was 30 years old and there was one child, Barbara, age 6.

Yancy Cade Carter died December 21, 1951. He was buried in Silver Brook Cemetery, Anderson, SC. There was a request for a head stone for military service with an enlistment date of June 11, 1898, and a discharge date of May 2, 1899. The date of service suggests he served during the Spanish-American War, probably in Cuba. There was a pension number of C 2 426 004. He was from SC with a rank of Sgt. serving in Third Regiment United States Infantry, Co. E. The request was signed by Nelle B. Carter, December 28, 1951.

William Yancey Carter

William Yancey Carter was born November 17, 1860, in Elberton, GA, the son of James M. Carter and Mary Louisa Clark. W. Y. Carter of Georgia enlisted in the Texas Rangers on March 1, 1881. He served for 7 months and 18 days receiving his discharge on October 19, 1881. He had light hair, hazel eyes and a light complexion. He served under Capt. G. W. Arrington, Front. Bat. Co. C. It did not take long after he returned to Georgia to get married. Yancey married Lucy Ella Sanders in Hart County on May 18, 1884.

W. Yancey Carter joined with his brother Florence M. Carter and his nephew Yancy Cade Carter in Company 'E', 3 U.S. Volunteer Infantry for service in the Spanish-American War in 1898. He was named a captain at the time he enlisted.

The family was located on the 1900 Georgia, Hart County census living in Alford District. W. Y. was noted as a farmer. There were five children in the home. There had been 7 children born to the family with only five living. The 1910 Florida, Polk County census locates the family where there was the addition of two more children. W. Y. was noted as a farmer. His wife was recorded as Lucy E. Carter, she was the parent of 9 children with 7 still living.

The family was found for the 1920 Florida census still living in Polk County, W. Y. Carter's occupation was given as Gen. Farm. There was a granddaughter Mary E. Carter, age 15, and five children named Hicks, Edma, age 12, Harley, age 9, Wiley, age 6, Hugh, age 4, and Lorena, age 1.

William Yancey Carter died on February 2, 1942, in Elizabeth City, at Langley Field, VA. He was buried in the Hampton National Cemetery because he was a veteran of the Spanish - American War, which probably meant the invasion of Cuba. The informant of the death certificate was Sarah C. Wilson, probably his daughter.

William Yancey Carter was the parent of seven known children

1. Gibson Carter
2. Yancey Carter
3. Ethel Carter
4. Caroline Carter
5. Clarence Carter
6. Emma S. Carter
7. Sarah Carter

James Monroe Carter Jr.

James M. Carter Jr. was born on January 29, 1865 in Hart County, GA, the son of James M. Carter Sr. and Mary Louisa Clark Carter. James married Mattie Virginia Estes daughter of William and Emma Mary Williford Estes in Hart County, GA on November 3, 1886. Mattie was born on February 26, 1872, in Georgia.

The family was located for the 1900 Georgia, Hart County census living in Alford under the name of Jim Carter. Jim was a farmer and there were seven children in the family. Also recorded in the home was Jim's father 79-year-old J. M. Carter.

The 1910 Georgia, Hart County census shows a change in some of the names and the addition of four more children to the family. William Carter was no longer in the home; Ola Carter had taken his place. Mattie Carter informed the census taker she was the mother of eleven children with eleven still living.

Mattie Virginia Estes Carter died on January 3, 1911. She was buried in Northview Cemetery, Hartwell, GA. James Monroe Carter Jr. died on June 14, 1914, he too was buried in Northview Cemetery, Hartwell, GA

Census listing in 1900, four added to the family for the 1910 census.

1. William Monroe Carter, age 13, died 1919
2. Ola Carter, age 10, later Thornton
3. Mack Carter, age 7
4. Marry Carter, age 6, became Marylou
5. Preston Brooks Carter, age 4, killed in the World War, 1918
6. Louina Carter, age 2, became Lourena
7. Berta Carter, age 0, became Nora
8. Anne Carter, age 8 in 1910
9. Emma Sue Carter, age 5, in 1910, later Gaines
10. Crystal Carter, age 3, in 1910
11. James B. Carter, age 1 or 1 and 8/12 in 1910.

Mack Alfred Carter

Mack Alfred Carter Sr. was born March 17, 1892, the son of James M. Carter, Jr. and Mattie Virginia Estes. Mack married Minnie Shiflet.

Mack's brother James B. Carter was living within this family for the 1920 census. He was 7 years old and noted as brother.

Mack A. Carter died April 19, 1969; he was buried in Cokesbury UMC Cemetery, Hart County, GA.

There were four children of this marriage.

1. Ellen Virginia Carter, later Mewborn
2. Mack Alfred Carter Jr.
3. Robbie Hugh Carter
4. Jimmy Alston Carter

David Carter Jr.

David Carter Jr. was born in Pendleton District, South Carolina on January 15, 1792, the son of David Carter Sr. and Mahitable Cobb Carter. It is believed that David served during the War of 1812, but no records have been found to support that fact.

David married Lavinia York on October 22, 1818, probably in Pendleton District, SC. Lavinia was born November 11, 1796 probably in the Pendleton District, SC. No information about her parents has been discovered. Lavinia York was known for telling stories about the Indians. She use to tell about visiting an Indian village or encampment in her youth where the Indians lived and plied their trade of making baskets and other things of Indian manufacture, gardening, hunting, fishing and other pursuits common to Indian life. Story told by James M. Carter in an article published in *The Hartwell Sun*, issue of September 19, 1902. Carter, a nephew to her husband, knew Lavinia very well.

"There was land between the high hills and the Savannah River which was in the early days a kind of Indian village, composed of huts, wigwams, and such other places of abode as they saw fit to construct and use for dwellings. Indian burying grounds where many of the Cherokee Indians are buried, signs of their graves may yet be seen," Carter continued in the article. With the signing of the 1830 Indian Removal Act by President Andrew Jackson, saw the removal of American Indians from Georgia.

David Carter Jr. was not found on the 1820 South Carolina or Georgia census. However, for the 1830 and 1840 Georgia census he was located in Franklin County. The family was located on the 1850 Georgia, Franklin County census. David was a fifty-five year old farmer with $200.00 worth of real estate property. Within the family enumeration was David's fifty-three year old wife Lavinia Carter and three children, David L. Carter, age 22, Harriett Carter, age 21, and Lavinia Carter, age 9. Who this 9 year old child belonged to is unknown but probably a grandchild.

The creation of Hart County, GA took place in 1853, taking portions from Franklin County and Elbert County. Lightwood Log Creek, where the Carters lived, was then placed entirely in Hart County. On April 5, 1856, David Carter and Lamarcus Carter sold to James M. Carter fifty-four acres of land situated on "little light wood creek" for $700.00. James M. Carter was noted as already living on the property.

David Carter Jr. died on March 10, 1859, during one of the worst typhoid fever epidemics known in the area that also took the lives of three of his children. David's son William Balus Carter was appointed executor of his estate but he died during the Civil War before the estate was settled. David Carter's brother Micajah Carter was then appointed executor after the war was over. David Carter Jr.'s assets consisted of land and one thousand dollars.

Lavinia Carter was found on the 1860 Georgia, Hart County census living in Dooley's District. Within this home was Lavinia Carter and below her name followed that of two of her children, John K. Carter, age 25, and Amanda Carter, age 20. Below Amanda's name followed that of Mary L. Carter, age 13, Susan A. Carter, age 11, Nancy F. Carter, age 9, Clury (f) Carter, age 4, Sarah L. Carter, age 8 and William W. Carter, age 6. Below William W. Carter's name was the name of James M. Carter, a 38 year old trader. It is believed the children named starting with Mary L. Carter were the children of the trader, James M. Carter.

The 1870 Georgia, Hart County census shows Lavinia Carter listed within the home of her son-in-law William Anderson Sanders who was married to Caroline Carter Sanders. Lavinia was not found in the Sander's home for the 1880 Hart County census.

Lavinia York Carter died on August 14, 1891. There was an obituary for Mrs. Carter, "Mrs. Vina Carter, an aged and most excellent Christian lady died last Friday at the home of her son-in-law, Mr. W. A. Sanders, in Alfords District. Aunt Vina as she was familiarly called by everyone in the neighborhood, was nearly one hundred years old, and had been a member of the Baptist Church for many years and lived a life of great usefulness. By her request, sometime before she died, Rev. T. A. Thornton preached the funeral at Mount Zion Church on Saturday, after which the feeble form of this good woman was laid to rest beside her loved ones gone before. Her grave is marked by a marble tombstone with the inscription;

Lavinia York Carter
Born Nov. 11, 1796
Married Oct. 22, 1818
Died Aug. 14, 1891

David and Lavinia Carter were both buried in Mount Zion Methodist graveyard, Hart County, GA. The remains of David and Lavinia and other family members were removed in 1961 and relocated at New Harmony Methodist. The removal of the remains was necessary because of the creation of a dam on the Savannah River. It is believed by certain family members some tombstones did not accompany the remains to the new location and are now under water.

David Carter Jr. and Lavinia York Carter were the parents of twelve known children.

1. Lamarcus E. Carter
2. James Madison Carter
3. Sarah Elizabeth Carter
4. Mary R. Carter
5. Riller Harriett Carter, born Feb. 13, 1826, died March 20, 1859*
6. David Louis Carter, born Jan. 28, 1828, died Jan. 26, 1859*
7. William Balus Carter, born Dec. 29, 1829, died 1865, Civil War
8. Elias Earle Carter, born April 21, 1831, died Feb. 12, 1834
9. Micajah K. Carter, born Oct. 17, 1832, died March 1859*
10. John K. Carter, born Dec. 18, 1834, died in 1866 in Louisiana
11. Elizabeth Ann Caroline Carter
12. Amanda B. Carter

* indicates death during the typhoid fever epidemic of 1859

Lamarcus E. Carter

Lamarcus E. Carter was born on August 16, 1819, in Pendleton District, SC, the son of David Carter Jr. and Lavinia York Carter. Lamarcus married ___ and they were the parents of three children. Lamarcus married for the second time to (Jane) Harriett Poole some time before 1850 and they had one child, Joel F. Carter.

Lamarcus Carter and family were located on the 1850 Georgia, Franklin County census recorded just before the family listing of his mother Lavinia Carter. Listed within the home was Marcus, a 29 year old farmer, his wife Jane H. Carter, age 20, Elizabeth Carter, age 10, Martha Carter, age 8, Nancy Carter, age 6 and a Rhonda Carter, age 27 years. Who Rhonda Carter was is unknown.

On April 5, 1856, Lamarcus Carter and David Carter sold to James M. Carter fifty-four acres of land described as the 'old Stoeker tract' and situated on 'little lightwood log creek' for $700.00. The deed noted James M. Carter was already living on the property.

The 1860 Georgia, Hart County census locates Lamarcus E. Carter recorded in the Dooley District. Lamarcus was a forty-one year old 'Millwright' with $750.00 worth of real estate property and $800.00 worth of personal property. His wife was recorded as Elizabeth M. H., age 26, the children listed were Mary E. Carter, age 18, Martha Carter, age 16, Louiza L. Carter, age 12 and Joel F. Carter, age 2.

Lamarcus died sometime between 1860 and 1870 because his wife was found as head of household for the 1870 Hart County census. She was listed as Harriett Carter, a farmer with $125.00 worth of real estate property. Below her name was that of her son Joel F. Carter and her mother Elizabeth Poole.

Information from the book *Hart County History,* states Lamarcus built a mill on Little Lightwood Creek that later became known as the Murry Place. He also built a sawmill on Gum Creek. This mill was later purchased by F. G. Stowers, who built and operated a flour and grist mill with a cotton gin on the site.

Lamarcus Carter was the parent of four known children.

1. Mary Elizabeth Carter, never married
2. Martha (Mattie)
3. Nancy (Lou)
4. Joel F. Carter

James Madison Carter

James Madison Carter was born in Pendleton District, SC on March 13, 1821, the son of David Carter Jr. and Lavinia York Carter. A biography of James M. Carter may be found in Section II starting on page 23.

Sarah Elizabeth Carter

Sarah Elizabeth Carter was born October 29, 1822, in Pendleton District, SC, the daughter of David Carter Jr. and Lavinia York Carter. Sarah married Richard N. Brown, the son of Nicholas Brown, and they had four children.

The family was found on the 1850 Georgia, Franklin County census. Richard was noted as a farmer from South Carolina. There were four children recorded in the family.

Sarah later married Elihu Hall and they had three children.

Sarah Carter Brown Hall was the parent of nine known children.

1. James Brown
2. Rhoda Brown
3. John Brown
4. William Brown
5. Eliza Brown
6. Ada Brown
7. Joel Turner Hall
8. Anderson D. Hall
9. Cora Hall

Mary R. Carter

Mary R. Carter was born February 12, 1824, in Pendleton District, SC, the daughter of David Carter Jr. and Lavinia York Carter. Mary married J. Garrison Richardson and moved to Alabama. Nothing more is known of this family.

Elizabeth Ann Caroline Carter

Elizabeth Ann Caroline Carter was born June 19, 1837, probably in Franklin County, Georgia, the daughter of David Carter Jr. and Lavinia York Carter. Elizabeth Ann, who appeared to prefer the name of Caroline, married William Anderson Sanders.

The 1860 Georgia, Hart County census shows this family listed just after the family listing of her mother. William A, Sanders was 25 years old, a lawyer, and Caroline N. Sanders was 23 years old and listed as 'Mrs.', there were no children in the home at that time.

The 1870 Georgia, Hart County census locates the family in Dooley's District. He was listed as Anderson Sanders, a 36 year old farmer. Caroline was 33 years old their children were as follows, Frances, age 9, Lucy S., age 7, Sarah C., age 4 and Albert P., age 2. Also living in the home was Lavinia Carter, Caroline's 73 year old mother.

The *Hart County History* book states Caroline Carter Sanders died on February 13, 1891. A few months later Lavinia York Carter died at the home of her son-in-law W. A. Sanders on August 14, 1891.

Elizabeth Carter Sanders and William A. Sanders were the parent of eight children.

1. Albert Perry Sanders
2. Florence Newton Sanders
3. John Harrison Sanders
4. Fannie Angeline Sanders
5. Lucy Ella Sanders
6. Sarah Caroline
7. Emma Alicia Sanders
8. Mornin Louisa Sanders

Amanda B. Carter

Amanda B. Carter was born October 23, 1839, in Franklin County, GA, the daughter of David Carter Jr. and Lavinia York Carter. Amanda married Thomas Pritchett. The family moved to Alabama where Amanda died in 1900.

There were two known children of this family.

1. Balus Pritchett
2. Sallie Lou Pritchett

PART II

James Madison Carter

James Madison Carter Sr. was born in Pendleton District, South Carolina at about 1823, the son of David Carter Jr. and Lavinia York Carter. James married Nancy Meason most likely in Franklin County, GA at about 1844. Nancy was also a native of South Carolina.

The James Madison Carter family was found for the 1850 Georgia census enumerated in Franklin County, GA. At this time James was noted as a 27-year-old farmer with $1,500 worth of real estate value. James's wife Nancy was recorded as 24 years old born in South Carolina. There were three children recorded in the home, they were Martha Carter, age 5, Jane Carter, age 3 and Rhoda Carter, age 1 year. All the children had been born in Georgia.

James M. Carter purchased 54 acres for $700.00 from Lamarcus Carter and David Carter on April 5, 1856. The land was described as the 'old Stoeker tract' lying on 'little light wood log creek' and bounded on the east by the lands of David Carter. The deed noted James M. Carter was already living on the property.

On January 27, 1858, James M. Carter sold the 54 acres tract of land described as the 'old Stoeker tract' to Micajah Carter for $800.00. This was the same property James had purchased from Lamarcus Carter and David Carter in 1856. This property according to John William Baker, author of *History of Hart County,* later became known as the 'old Elias Vickery home place.' The sale of this property was probably in preparations for the James M. Carter family leaving the state of Georgia moving to Louisiana.

It is believed that Nancy Meason Carter died in Hart County, GA in 1859 during a severe typhoid fever epidemic. Nancy's father-in-law David Carter Jr. and three of his children also perished during this terrible epidemic. There are, however, other research sources that suggest Nancy may have died in route to Louisiana or just after she arrived there.

Hart County, GA was created on February 6, 1856, taking parts of Franklin County and Elbert County and combining them. The 1860 Hart County census shows James M. Carter recorded within the home of his mother Lavinia Carter. His occupation was recorded as 'Trader' not as a Slave trader as quoted by some other family researchers. There were six children in the home who appear to be the children of James M. Carter. The children were, Mary L. Carter, age 13, Susan A. Carter, age 11, Nancy F. Carter, age 9, Clury (f) A. Carter, age 4, Sarah L. Carter, age 8 and William W. Carter, age 6.

James M. Carter married Frances Ann Coats on May 24, 1860, in the Catahoula Parrish, Louisiana. James signed the marriage license which at the time cost $3.00. Frances was born in Mississippi in September 1840, James was 39 years old while Frances was 19. Catahoula Parrish borders the western banks of the Mississippi River, midway between Vicksburg, MS and Baton Rouge, LA. Natchez, MS is located on the opposite bank of the Mississippi River from the Catahoula Parrish. The seat of the Catahoula Parrish is Harrisonburg, LA.

Frances Coats Carter

The Coats family is known to have been living in Catahoula Parrish during the time of the 1850 and 1860 Louisiana census. Frances is known to have had an older sister named Catherine Coats who was born in Georgia in September 1836, and two brothers, George Coats and William J. Coats. Catherine's mother and father were both born in South Carolina. The Coats family, who had roots in both South Carolina and Georgia, appear to have moved to Louisiana about the year 1839 or 1840. It seems highly probable that James M. Carter knew the Coats family both in South Carolina and Georgia. That would be one of the reasons why he married a woman of her background so soon after the death of his first wife.

Although James M. Carter was married in Louisiana, he may have had some kind of connection to Mississippi. This fact is suggested because when he joined the Confederate Army, he joined in Mississippi not Louisiana. James joined the First Regular Mississippi Light Artillery as a 41-year-old private on April 10, 1862, at Lexington, MS for a period of "three years or war." This unit was also known as Wither's Light Artillery. The regiment was assembled at an encampment near Jackson, MS in May 1862. In January 1863, the regiment was listed as part of Gen. S.D. Lee's command at Vicksburg.

Corporal James M. Carter of Company 'D' of the 1st Regular Mississippi Light Artillery was captured at the capitulation of Vicksburg to the Union Army under the command of Gen. U.S. Grant on July 4, 1863. At that time, he was under the command of Lieut. Gen. John C. Pemberton. On the 7th of July 1863, James signed a parole agreement with the U.S. government, stating he would not "take up arms against the United States." He was sent to Demopolis, Alabama where he was placed on the rolls of Co 'F' 1st. Detached Paroled Prisoners. James was at this camp until August 1864. In September 1864, he left camp, apparently exchanged and was soon back in his old unit. James appears to have been promoted to Sergeant shortly after this time.

After July 1864, Company 'D' was sent to Mobile, AL doing provost duty there. The Mobile Battalion was ordered to Blakely, AL, where they served during the siege by Gen. Canby. Following a period of fierce fighting the garrison was finally surrendered. Military service records state Serge. James M. Carter was captured again on April 9, 1865, at Blakely, AL. He was then sent to Ship Island, MS and later transferred to Vicksburg, MS on May 1, 1865.

A Carter family legend suggest Frances Coats Carter may have been living in Vicksburg during the terrible 1863 siege. This may have been because she wanted to be near her husband, but it could have been because this was where her Coats family lived.

It appears the James M. Carter Sr. family moved to Texas at about 1867. A family story states that following the war James left by boat for New Orleans then moving on to Freestone County, TX. Credence is given to this story when it was discovered that settlers could take a ship to Galveston, then transfer to a lighter craft and travel up the Trinity River all the way to Navarro Landing north of Freestone County. There is also a family story that for a time James operated a ferry across the Trinity River between Palestine, TX and Fairfield, TX. The 1870 census show the family was living at the post office address of Fairfield. However, the 1870 census records James occupation as farmer.

The 1870 census records show there were four children listing that are believed to be from James's first marriage. These children were Nancy L. Carter, age 19, Sarah S. Carter, age 17, Carrie L. Carter, age 15 and a male child listed as M.P.(Micajah P.) Carter, age 16. James and Frances were the parents of two boys at that time, J. M (James Madison), age 3, born in Louisiana and D. L.(David Louis) Carter, age 2, born in Texas.

The James M. Carter family was listed on-line item 33 of the 1870 Freestone County census while on-line item 34 was the family of Benjamin B. Bonner and his wife Mary Lavinia Carter Bonner. This was the family of James's oldest daughter Mary from his first marriage.

James M. Carter Sr. died in 1879 and was buried in Butler, Freestone County, TX. The county records for Freestone County do not show James M. Carter ever owning any property in the county.

The Frances A. Carter family was found for the 1880 Texas census living in Leon County. Frances was noted as a widow with an occupation of a farmer. There were five children in the home at this time, James M. Carter, age 13 David L. Carter, age 12, Frances(f) A. Carter, age 9, Benjamin F. Carter, age 8, and Robert J. Carter, age 6. James's place of birth was Louisiana while the other children's birthplaces were all in Texas. A review of the families located near the Carter family shows several Coats families. There was a William J. Coats family and a George W. Coats family. The George W. Coats family contain a listing for Catherine Coats, probable sister of Frances A. Carter.

The 1900 Texas census, Limestone County shows Frances A. Carter living within the home of her son James M. Carter. Frances was 59 years old with the census records saying she had been the parent of six children with five still alive. The family listed next to James M. Carter was his sister Fannie Carter Eldridge and her husband Frank. Several listings later were Dave (David) Carter with his wife Eugenia and their three children, Claude, Mamie and Ora. Also in the home was an aunt named Catherine Coats who was born in Georgia in September 1836. To round out this family was Dave's younger brother Ben Carter.

For the 1910 Texas census McLennan County, Frances A. Carter was found enumerated within the home of her son James M. Carter. Also listed in the home was her sister Catherine Coats. There were also two grandchildren listed Mamie Carter and Robert Carter, children of David Louis Carter who died in 1902.

Frances Coats Carter's death has been given as 1914 with her place of death being near Waco, TX. Frances lived for 35 years as a widow. It fell to her to raise five young children alone. Certainly not an easy task.

The exact number of James Madison Carter's children from his first marriage to Nancy Meason is not known with certainty. Family researchers have listed Mary Lavinia Carter as a possible child of Nancy Meason. Mary married Benjamin B. Bonner at the home of James M. Carter Sr. in Catahoula Parrish, LA on July 20, 1867.

With the exception of the already mentioned Mary Lavinia Carter and a Nancy L. Carter, only the children from James's second marriage with Frances Ann Coats can be covered in this research effort with any certainty. James M. Carter Sr. and Frances Ann Coats were the parents of five known children. James is believed to have been the father of at least six additional children with his first wife Nancy Meason.

1. Mary Lavinia Carter
2. Susan A. Carter, born 1949
3. Nancy L. Carter, born 1851
4. Sarah L. Carter
5. William W. Carter, born 1854
6. Clary A. Carter, born 1856
7. James M. Carter Jr.
8. David Louis Carter
9. Frances Ann Carter
10. Benjamin Franklin Carter
11. Robert Carter, born in 1874, died in 1893, no issue

Mary Lavinia Carter

Mary Lavinia Carter was born in Georgia on August 17, 1847, the daughter of James M. Carter Sr. and his first wife Nancy Meason Carter. She was apparently was named in honor of her grandmother Lavinia York Carter. It is unclear how many of James's children with his first wife moved to Louisiana then to Texas with their father. Mary appears to be one of them.

Mary L. Carter married Benjamin Beck Bonner in Mansfield, Louisiana on July 20, 1867. Benjamin had served with Company 'A', 71st Regiment Louisiana Infantry. He joined the regiment on April 26, 1862 and was captured when Vicksburg fell on July 4, 1863. He was sent to Camp Norton, Indianapolis, Indiana. There he joined the Union Army, serving as a blacksmith. While he served on both sides of the war, he never fought against his Southern brothers. When he joined the Union Army, he dropped his surname becoming Benjamin Beck.

A child named Lillie (Frances L.) was born in Louisiana in 1868. In 1870, the family was found on census in Fairfield, Freestone County, TX living very close to her father's home. There was one child recorded in the home at that time, Frances L. Bonner, who was two years old. Another child was a fifteen-year-old Ellen L. Bonner who proved to be the sister to Benjamin Bonner. The Bonner family was found on the 1860 Parrish of Morehouse, Bastrop Post Office, headed by A. Bonner, a 45-year-old blacksmith from Mississippi.

In 1880, the family was found living in Limestone County, TX, there were four children listed at that time, Frances L, Benj. B., James A. and Pearl A. B. B. Bonner was a 36-year-old farmer. A child named Julia Ellen Bonner was born to the family on September 16, 1880, in Anderson County, TX.

In November of 1884, at the time when Mollie Bonner was born, the family was living in Mexia, the county seat of Limestone County, TX. There was no doctor in the community, so Benjamin and Mary traveled to Kerans, Navarro County, TX where the baby was delivered. The next night Benjamin B. Bonner expired while in the bed with his wife and their new baby. The doctor said his death was most likely caused by "acute indigestion," but most probably it was caused by a case of rupture appendicitis.

The people of Kerans nursed Mary back to health and took her home to Mexia with the new baby. Nearly destitute, Mary turned to and was refused help from two Bonner bachelor uncles of her husband. An elderly-colored couple, who lived nearby offered the family help and shared their ten-acre garden space with Mary. Other neighbors helped, but the family barely survived.

Nearly two and a half years later, about 1886 or 1887, a young man by the name of John M. Philips came to East Texas to buy cattle for a Vernon, TX banker. When he heard about the pretty widow with five children, he became curious and called on the family. A family story goes that when John arrived at the home, he found all the children suffering with measles. So, John went and purchased bacon and other food and took it to them and offered his help. There was a dance being held that night, so he asked Mary to go with him. She surprised him by saying yes. On the way home from the dance, he asked her to marry him, and she did. They were married one week later.

Originally John had come to court Mary's daughter Lilly but ended up marrying Mary and taking the whole family back with him to Medicine Mounds, Hardeman County, TX.

Following their marriage John and Mary and the entire Bonner family drove the cattle on a three - month adventure that ended with the family having Christmas dinner in the wagon yard at Wichita Falls, TX. The cattle drive which included two oxen drawn covered wagons, had survived swollen creeks, river crossings and an Indian hunting party that took only three of their cattle. John, who was sixteen years younger than Mary, surprised many friends when he arrived back home with a rather large intact family. John Marion Philips was born in Rutherford County, TN on April 22, 1863, the son of John Philips and Lackey Crawford. John was a big man, 6'4" inches tall and weighing 220 pounds.

The John M. Philips family was found on the 1900 Texas census Hardeman County. The census offers important information like birthdays for family members. John M. Philips was born in April 1863, in Tennessee, Mary L. was born in Georgia in August 1848, Mollie Bonner was born in Texas in October 1884, Clifford Philips was born in Texas in August 1890. There was also a Mary Nickles noted as a granddaughter, born in Texas in June 1894.

The family moved to Groesbeck, Limestone County, TX in 1911. John M. Philips died of diabetes mellitus on Monday, April 20, 1925. The informant for the death certificate was Mrs. John M. Philips of Quanah, TX. He was buried in Quanah Cemetery, Hardeman County, TX.

Mary Bonner Philips was found for the 1930 Texas census, Foard County, in the city of Crowell living with her daughter Pearl who was the wife of Lewis Kamster. Pearl appeared to not have any children of her own only stepchildren. Mary died of acute bronchitis on December 3, 1932. The informant for the death certificate was J. B. LaRus(?) of Margaret, TX.

Mary gave on the 1900 census information that she was the mother of 7 children with 6 still living. These six would have include her son Clifford Philips. So, she was the parent of five children with Benjamin Bonner and one child with John M Philips.

1. Frances Lillie Bonner
2. Benjamin B. Bonner
3. James A. Bonner
4. Pearl A. Bonner
5. Julia Ellen Bonner
6. Mollie Bonner
7. Clifford Philips

Frances Lillie Bonner

Frances Lillie Bonner was born in Louisiana in 1868, the daughter of Mary Lavinia Carter and Benjamin Beck Bonner.

Benjamin Beck Bonner Jr.

Benjamin Beck Bonner Jr. was born in Texas in 1874, the son of Mary Lavinia Carter and Benjamin Beck Bonner Sr.

Ben was married to Estelle Kellis, they were the parents of five children. He then married Quilla Brisco Phillips and they had three children. Ben was a "sooth sayer." He did readings from Coffee grounds in his cup. He was a kind and gentle man, a farmer and prospector. His children live in Arizona and California.

James A. Bonner

James A. Bonner was born in Texas in 1878, the son of Mary Lavinia Carter and Benjamin Beck Bonner. Jim was a charmer. He had traveled to South America and worked in gem mines there. He was prospector living most of his life in New Mexico and Arizona. His wife's name was Hannah, they had two daughters.

Pearl A. Bonner

Pearl A. Bonner was born in Texas in 1879, the daughter of Mary Lavinia Carter and Benjamin Beck Bonner.

Julia Ellen Bonner

Julian Ellen Bonner was born at Palestine, Anderson County, TX on September 16, 1880, the daughter of Mary L. Carter and Benjamin B. Bonner.

Julia married Harry Eugene Cobb on September 16, 1899, in Chillicothe, Hardeman County, TX. Harry was born October 26, 1878, in Wichita, Kansas, the son of Henry Clay Cobb and Mary Ellen Smith.

Harry's father, Henry Clay Cobb, came to live with the family where his grandson Leslie C. Cobb learned much of his family's history. Henry Clay Cobb was born in London, Iowa, on October 23, 1846. It seems Henry's father John S. Cobb had come into this country at Boston, Mass. John S. Cobb of English and Welsh parents moved on to New York where he met and married Laura Spencer. They moved to London, Iowa where they proceeded to have thirteen children.

The Cobb family was living in Wichita, KS where Henry Clay Cobb met and married Mary Ellen Smith on December 23, 1877. Mary was born in Milwaukee, Wisconsin on September 26, 1859, the daughter of Mr. and Mrs. John Charles Smith, who had come to Wichita from Milwaukee. The Henry Clay Cobb family moved to Kansas City, Missouri and a few years later they moved to Vernon, TX. Henry was a commercial building contractor and spent much of his time in Dallas. The family later purchased a farm in Tolbert, Hardeman County, TX.

After Grandfather Cobb passed on, Grandmother Mary Lavinia Carter Bonner Philips came to live with the family. She told the story how the Carters had come into this country at New England but moved on to New Jersey. Then the family moved to Georgia, then to Mississippi, then to Louisiana and then on to Texas. She went on to say Benjamin Beck Bonner was a schoolteacher, a dancing teacher and a hero for the Confederacy. His occupation was a blacksmith.

There were two children of this marriage.

1. Leslie Clyde Cobb
2. Clois Raymond Cobb

Leslie Clyde Cobb

Leslie Clyde Cobb was born in Hardeman County, TX on August 17, 1913, the son of Harry Eugene Cobb and Julia Ellen Bonner. His birth was registered at the historic county seat, Quanah, TX.

Leslie married Ruthell Clark at Crowell, Foard County, TX on June 25, 1939. Foard County is located due south of Hardeman County.

Leslie Cobb wrote a paper on part of the Carter Family history and visited the home place in Hart County, GA on five different occasions.

Leslie and Ruthell Clark were the parents of two sons.

1. John Eugene Cobb
2. Randall Leslie Cobb

John Eugene Cobb

John Eugene Cobb was born at Fort Worth, Tarrant County, TX on April 7, 1948, the son of Leslie Clyde Cobb and Ruthell Clark.

John married Melinda K. Swihart on August 5, 1867. They are the parents of two children.

1. Tamara Keye Cobb, born October 24, 1969
2. Jennifer Jaye Cobb, born August 15, 1973

Randall Leslie Cobb

Randall Leslie Cobb was born at Midland, Midland County, TX on March 25, 1955, the son of Leslie Clyde Cobb and Ruthell Clark Cobb.

Clois Raymond Cobb

Clois Raymond Cobb was born at Vernon, Wibarger County, TX on January 17, 1920, the son of Harry Eugene Cobb and Julia Ellen Bonner. The number of children from this family is unknown, but one child is suspected

1. Clois Raymond Cobb Jr.

Mollie Bonner

Mollie Bonner was born in Karnes, TX in October 1884, the daughter of Mary Lavinia Carter and Benjamin Beck Bonner. Mollie was born the day before her father died.

Clifford Philips

Clifford Philips was born in Texas in August 1890, the son of Mary Lavinia Carter Bonner Philips and John M. Philips.

Cliff died young, but had a son also named Cliff who has many descendants. Cottonwood, Arizona had a number of Cliff's descendants

Nancy L. Carter

Nancy L. Carter was born in Georgia in 1851, the daughter of James Madison Carter Sr. and Nancy Meason, she was found in the home of her father for the 1870 Freestone County, TX census. She was then 19 years old. Nancy married James Strickland in Freestone County, TX on November 3, 1872

James Madison Carter Jr.

James Madison Carter Jr. was born on May 14, 1867, in Mississippi, probably near Vicksburg, MS the son of James Madison Carter Sr. and Frances Coats Carter. James was found with the family for the 1870 Freestone County, TX census. For the 1880 Texas census, he was with his family headed by his mother living in Leon County. He was only 13 years old and listed as a farmer.

James married Mattie Eugenia Irene Rutherford in Freestone County, TX on December 31, 1891. Mattie, known as Irene or Renie, was born on June 8, 1874, in Llano, TX, the daughter of Shelton Lindsey Rutherford and Josephine Powell Rutherford. Mr. Rutherford was born in Arkansas while Mrs. Rutherford was born in Tennessee.

The 1900 Texas census, Limestone County show the family living in Justice Precinct # 2. Recorded in the home was James and his wife Rene with their four children, Ollie, Franklin, Obed and Matte. James's mother Frances A. Carter was also found in the home.

James Madison Carter, Jr.

The 1910 Texas census, McLennan County records the family living in Justice Precinct #2. James M. Carter Jr. and his wife Irene and their seven children were enumerated. The children were Ollie, Frank, Obed, Mattie, Leola, Allie (Alice) and Clyde Carter. Also listed in the home were Mamie Carter and Robert Carter, children of David Louis Carter; his brother who died in 1902. His mother Fannie (Frances Ann) Carter and her sister Catherine Coats were also found in the home. There were thirteen people living in the household at this time.

James Madison Carter Jr. died at the young age of 49 years on February 2, 1917, in Otto, TX. He was buried at Mart, TX cemetery. With the death of her husband, Irene Rutherford Carter, like her mother-in-law Frances Coats Carter, would be called upon to raise and mature her young family alone. These two women never wavered from the task of keeping their families together against awesome odds. The Carter family, for two generations, owes a great debt to the steadfast character and devotion to family of Frances Coats Carter and Irene Rutherford Carter.

The 1920 Texas Limestone County census, Justice Precinct #8, shows Irene's son Obed Carter listed as head of household. Irene was listed next followed by the other children Frank, Cleo, Alice and Shirley Carter. The family listed following Irene's family was her sister Olivia Rutherford Ashabranner and her husband Carl and their six children. The family listed after Olivia's family was Shelton and Josephine Rutherford, Irene and Olivia's parents.

Irene's grandson, Sherwood Johnson Carter, remembered her as the sweetest, gentlest woman he had ever known. She used to come for long visits to Sherwood's family in Hobbs, NM, when the summer became too hot in Waco where she lived.

The Waco newspaper *Times-Herald,* dated Monday, September 27, 1948, under the 'Funeral Notices' section shows "Mrs. Irene Carter, 74, 1523 North Thirteenth Street, died in a local hospital at 2:25 am Monday. The short article also mentioned she was survived by three daughters, Mrs. Cleo Clampett of Waco, Mrs. Alice Gibson of Waco and Mrs. Shirley Stephenson of Gardenia, Calif. There were two sons mentioned, O.J. Carter of Groesbeck and Frank Carter of Hobbs, N.M. Mrs. Carter's sister, Mrs. Olivia Ashabranner of Waco was also recorded. Mrs. Carter was buried in the cemetery at Mart, TX.

James Madison Carter Jr. and Rene Rutherford Carter were the parents of nine known children.

1. Ollie Bell Carter
2. Franklin Eli Carter
3. John Obed Carter
4. Mattie Ann Carter
5. Laura Cleo Carter
6. Ruby Pearl Carter, born Dec. 22, 1903, died May 14, 1905
7. Alice Viola Carter
8. Clyde Collom Carter, born 1909, died 1917
9. Shirley Ruth Carter

Ollie Bell Carter

Ollie Bell Carter was born on January 21, 1893, in Limestone County, TX, the daughter of James Madison Carter Jr. and Mattie (Rene) Rutherford Carter. Ollie married John A. Olson.

The family was found for the 1930 Texas, Limestone County census. The family was living on Park Street. There were two children in the home, Charles and Irene J. Olson. Also in the home were Ollie's sister Shirley R. Carter and their mother Mattie E. Carter. John Olson's father John Olson was also in the household.

Ollie died on December 28, 1932; she was buried in the Mart Cemetery, Mart, TX.

Ollie Carter and John Olson were the parents of two known children.

1. Charles Olson
2. Irene J. Olson

Franklin Eli Carter

Franklin Eli Carter was born at Keechie, Freestone County, TX, on April 29, 1894, the son of James Madison Carter Jr. and Mattie (Rene) Rutherford Carter. A biography of the Franklin Carter family may be found in Section III, page number 43.

ohn Obed Carter

John Obed Carter was born on September 8, 1896, the son of James Madison Carter Jr. and Mattie (Rene) Rutherford Carter. John, known as Obed, married Velma Brown.

The 1930 Texas census, Limestone County, Justice Precinct #3 shows this family under the name of O.J. Carter. The family rented the property and O.J. Carter was a farmer.

Obed Carter died May 9, 1964, he was buried at Big Hill, TX.

Obed Carter and Vera Brown Carter were the parents of three known children.

1. Johnnie Carter(f)
2. Marcus Carter
3. James Carter

Mattie Ann Carter

Mattie Ann Carter was born on September 26, 1898, the daughter of James Madison Carter Jr. and Mattie (Rene) Rutherford Carter. Mattie married Carlton Nichols. Mattie died in an automobile accident in Fort Worth, TX on April 3 1930, she was buried in Mart, TX cemetery. Two known children.

1. Leo Carter Nichols
2. Leldon Nichols, died result being run over by a car about 1925

Laura Cleo Carter

Laura Cleo Carter was born October 7, 1901, the daughter of James Madison Carter Jr. and Mattie (Rene) Rutherford Carter. Laura known as Cleo, married Frank Dean Clampitt on December 24, 1927. Frank died January 24, 1980.

Alice Viola Carter

Alice Viola Carter was born on September 27, 1906, the daughter of James Madison Carter Jr. and Mattie (Rene) Rutherford Carter. Alice married John Robert Gibson on December 3, 1927. Alice died in May 1986.

Shirley Ruth Carter

Shirley Ruth Carter was born February 22, 1916, the daughter of James Madison Carter Jr. and Mattie (Rene) Rutherford. Shirley married George Leroy Stevenson on September 5, 1937.

Shirley and her nephew Sherwood Carter Sr. owned a restaurant in San Diego, CA.

David Louis Carter

David (Dave) Louis Carter was born in Texas in January 1869, the son of James Madison Carter Sr. and Frances Coats Carter. David married Eugenia Ann Day on July 13, 1891, Leon county, TX.

The David L. Carter family was found on the 1900 Texas, Limestone County, census living very near his other family members. There were three children in the home at this time, Claude, Mamie and Ora. Also in the home was David's aunt Catherine Coats. David and Eugenia had been married nine years and three of their four children were still living. David was a farmer.

David died on December 22, 1902, he was buried in Mart cemetery, Mart, TX. Eugenia Day Carter died on March 21, 1903. She was also buried in the Mart, TX cemetery. For the 1910 McLennan County, TX census, Mamie and Robert Carter were living within the home of their uncle James M. Carter Jr. and his rather large family. Where the other children were at this time is unknown.

1. Claude Wallace Carter, born Sept. 1893
2. Mamie Ann Carter, born May 1896
3. Ora Bell Carter, born July 1898
4. Robert Jackson Carter, born 1901
5. Lewis David Carter, born 1903

Claude Wallace Carter

Claude Wallace Carter was born on September 21, 1893, the son of David Louis Carter and Eugenia Day Carter. Claude married Prudy Myrl Westbrook.

Mamie Ann Carter

Mamie Ann Carter was born in May 1896, the daughter of David Louis Carter and Eugenia Day Carter.

Ora Bell Carter

Ora Bell Carter was born in July 1898, the daughter of David Louis Carter and Eugenia Day Carter.

Robert Jackson Carter

Robert Jackson Carter was born March 21, 1903, the son of David Louis Carter and Eugenia Day Carter. Robert married Lucy Mae Bethurem, they were the parents of three children.

1. David Horace Carter
2. Mildred Carter
3. Dorothy Lee Carter

Dorothy Lee Carter

Dorothy Lee Carter was born in Canyon, TX on November 19, 1932, the daughter of Robert Jackson Carter and Lucy Mae Bethurem. Dorothy married Jerre Reagan Inman. He was born March 18, 1931.

Dorothy and Jerre were the parents of four children.

1. Rebecca Ann Inman
2. Randall Lee Inman
3. Tommy Dale Inman
4. Carter Lynn Inman, born Jan. 24, 1965, in Lamar, Colorado

Rebecca Ann Inman

Rebecca Ann Inman was born April 10, 1954, in Canyon, TX, the daughter of Dorothy Lee Carter and Jerre Reagan Inman. Rebecca has one child.

1. Ashlee Daiele Inman, born Jan. 25, 1979, in Odessa, TX

Randall Lee Inman

Randall Lee Inman was born May 23, 1955, in Canyon, TX, the son of Dorothy Lee Carter and Jerre Reagan Inman. Randall married Victoria Ann Hicks. She was born March 3, 1957, in Midland, TX. They are the parents of two children.

1. Jeramy David Inman, born June 28, 1976, in Midland, TX
2. Zacharey Lee Inman, born June 18, 1980, in Midland, TX

Tommy Dale Inman

Tommy Dale Inman was born June 22, 1957, in Canyon, TX, the son of Dorothy Lee Carter and Jerre Reagan Inman. Tommy married Courtney Ann O'Hearn. She was born February 28, 1959, in Fort Worth, TX. They are the parents of two children.

1. Thomas Price Inman, born August 14, 1981, Midland, TX
2. Hunter Inman, born April 7, 1984, Midland, TX

Lewis David Carter

Lewis David Carter was born on March 17, 1903, the son of David Louis Carter and Eugenia Day Carter. Tragically, Lewis's mother died four days after his birth which had been preceded four months earlier when his father died.

Lewis married Ruby Elizabeth _____, she was born August 20, 1903, the daughter of _____.

Lewis David Carter died august 20, 1984, Ruby died September 18, 1989; both are buried in the Mart Cemetery, Mart, TX.

Frances Ann Carter

Frances Ann Carter was born in Texas in 1870, the daughter of James Madison Carter Sr. and Frances Coats Carter. Frances married H. Clark Eldridge about the year 1895, she was then 15 years old. He was born in 1864.

H. Clark Eldridge and his wife Fanny were found on the 1930 Texas, Dickens County census, Justice Precinct #1, living in the town of McAdoo. Within this home was listed their granddaughter Laura Eldridge Simmons and her husband Laurence Simmons, one year old child named Laurence Simmons. Their daughter Ola Eldridge Wallace and her husband Rufus Wallace and their daughter Bessie M. Wallace were also recorded in the home.

On this same census living close by were three of Clark and Fanny's sons, Willie, Norman and Ben Eldridge.

H. Clark Eldridge died in 1948, Frances died in 1952.

H. Clark Eldridge and Frances Ann Carter were the parents of six known children.

1. Willie Eldridge
2. Ola Eldridge
3. Norman C. Eldridge
4. Jin Eldridge, born November 1894
5. Edgar Eldridge, born August 1896, died early
6. Benjamin Franklin Eldridge

Willie Eldridge

Willie Eldridge was born in Limestone County, TX in September 1887, the son of Frances A. Carter and H. Clark Eldridge. Willie married Lillie Mae _____, she was born on April 11, 1895.

In 1930, this family was found in Dickens County, living in the town of McAdoo. There was one child recorded in the home for that census year.

1. Francis L. Eldridge, age 16 in 1930

Ola Eldridge

Ola Eldridge was born in Limestone County, TX in November 1888, the daughter of Frances A. Carter and H. Clark Eldridge. Ola married Rufus Wallace about 1908 probably in Limestone County, TX.

Ola died on November 4, 1975 and is buried in McAdoo Cemetery. Death reported by her daughter Mrs. Raymond Harris.

They were the parents of two known children.

Norman C. Eldridge

Norman C. Eldridge was born in Limestone County, TX in February 1891, the son of Frances Ann Carter and H. Clark Eldridge. Norman married Willie L. ____, she was born about the year 1893.

Norman was located on the 1930 Texas, Dickens County census. Recorded within the listing was his wife Willie L., age 37 years. Included within the home were daughters Ruby Eldridge, age 18 and Maria Eldridge, age 17. Maria's husband Lawrence Fox and their child Joyce M. Fox, age 2 1/2 were also included in the family listing.

Norman died in 1960, Willie L. died in 1964. Both are buried in McAdoo, TX

Norman and his wife were the parents of two known children.

1. Ruby Eldridge
2. Maria Eldridge

Benjamin Franklin Eldridge

Benjamin F. Eldridge was born on March 6, 1899, in Limestone County, TX, the son of Frances A. Carter and H. Clark Eldridge. He was found with his family for the 1900 Limestone County census. Ben married Ollie Lee Phifer on June 28, 1925. She was born September 26, 1902.

Benjamin Franklin and Ollie Lee Eldridge

Ben was found on the 1930 Dickens County census living in the town of McAdoo, TX living very near to other members of his family. There was a small child, a daughter named Alhoe G. Eldridge listed at this time.

Ollie died August 26, 1980, Benjamin F. Eldridge died November 14, 1992, both are buried at McAdoo cemetery.

1. Alhoe G. Eldridge

Benjamin Franklin Carter

Benjamin Franklin Carter was born in Freestone County, TX on November 19, 1873, the son of James Madison Carter Sr. and Frances Coats Carter. Ben was found on the 1880 Leon County, TX census within the household headed by his mother Frances Coats Carter. He was found listed within the home of his brother David Carter for the 1900 Limestone County, TX census.

Ben married Maude Ann Rutherford probably in Limestone County about the year 1909. Maude was born January 4, 1892, the daughter of David A. Rutherford and M. Laurissa Day. Maude was a first cousin to Mattie Eugenia Irene Rutherford, wife of Ben's older brother James M. Carter Jr.

The 1920 Texas, Limestone County census, Justice precinct #8 records this family. Ben was a farmer with four children, he rented his property. Listed with his family was a brother-in-law named Home, probably Homer Rutherford. Home was a 28 year old farmer.

The 1930 Texas, Limestone census, Justice Precinct #8 enumerates this family. There were four children in the household, the children's names are listed below as is Ben's father -in-law Dave

39

Rutherford. Mr. Rutherford was 81 years old stating he had been born in Tennessee. His father was noted as being born in Kentucky while his mother was born in Mississippi.

Ben died May 23, 1945, he was buried in the cemetery at Mart, TX. Maude Ann Rutherford Carter died February 3, 1977. She was also buried in the Mart, TX cemetery.

Ben Carter and Maude Rutherford Carter were the parents of four known children.

1. Ruby Alberta Carter
2. Arvel Gillam Carter
3. Durwood Carter
4. Geneva Carter

Ruby Alberta Carter

Ruby Alberta Carter was born May 24, 1909, the daughter of Benjamin Carter and Maude Ann Rutherford Carter. Ruby married James Wilson Bennett on August 10, 1956. He was born November 18, 1913.

Arvel Gillam Carter

Arvel Gillam Carter was born December 30, 1910, the son of Benjamin Carter and Maude Rutherford Carter. Arvel Carter married Juanita Gunn in September 1934. She was born May 15, 1918. Three known children.

1. Jacqueline Carter
2. Arvel Lee Carter
3. Elizabeth Ann Carter

Jacqueline Carter

Jacqueline Carter was born January 19, 1941, the daughter of Arval Carter and Juanita Gunn. Jacqueline Carter married Harold Wayne Vaughn. He was born April 17, 1937. There were two children born of this marriage.

1. Melinda Vaughn, br. Jan. 23, 1959, married Steve P. Samples, one child Lance Wayne Samples, br. Oct. 16, 1981
2. Wayne Glenn Vaughn, born June 28, 1963

Arvel Lee Carter

Arvel Lee Carter was born June 19, 1943, the son of Arvel Carter and Juanita Gunn. Arvel married Patricia Fortenberry. She was born December 20, 1940. There was one child of this marriage.

1. Suzanne Lee Carter

Elizabeth Ann Carter

Elizabeth Ann Carter was born January 21, 1957, the daughter of Arvel G. Carter and Juanita Gunn. Elizabeth married Rick Grant and next married Billy Bob Walker. They have two children.

1. Rhett Carter Walker, born Nov. 9, 1979
2. Amanda Walker, born Nov. 19, 1981

Durwood Carter

Durwood Carter was born October 21, 1912, the son of Benjamin Carter and Maude Ann Rutherford. Durwood married Betty Aileen Hood on August 9, 1936. There are two children of this marriage.

1. Larissa Mae Carter
2. Mark Alan Carter

Larissa Mae Carter

Larissa Mae Carter was born December 29, 1937, the daughter of Durwood Carter and Betty Aileen Hood. Larissa married Robert Malcolm Struwe, they have two children.

1. Robert Carter Struwe, born Dec. 14, 1963
2. Milissa Lue Struwe, born Aug. 14, 1965

Geneva Carter

Geneva Carter was born November 23, 1914, the daughter of Benjamin Carter and Maude Ann Rutherford. Geneva married Esquire T. Hood on November 23, 1935. He was born January 13, 1913, in Nettleton, Miss.

Esquire Hood died March 12, 1977; there were two children of this marriage.

1. David Charles Hood
2. Judy Elaine Hood

David Charles Hood

David Charles Hood was born December 14, 1938, the son of Geneva Carter and Esquire T. Hood. David married Gloria Gardenshire, she was born August 21, 1941. They were the parents of three children.

1. David Charles Hood Jr., born Dec. 13, 1960. Married Cynthia Dawn Kierum
2. John Burt Hood, born April 4, 1963. Married Kathy Sue Dietrich
3. Andrew Carter Hood, born Oct. 27, 1966

Judy Elaine Hood

Judy Elaine Hood was born August 14, 1943, the daughter of Geneva Carter and Esquire Hood. Judy married John A. Coats; they have two children.

1. Jennifer Elizabeth Coats, born Feb. 23, 1964. Married Larry Wayne Fickel
2. John Coats, born August 23, 1966

PART III

Franklin Eli Carter

Franklin Eli Carter was born in Keechi, Freestone County, TX on April 29, 1894, the son of James Madison Carter Jr. and Mattie Rene Rutherford. He was found within the family listed under the name of his father for the 1900 Texas, Limestone County census in Precinct #2. Franklin's grandmother, Frances Coats Carter was also recorded in the home.

The 1910 Texas McLennan County census shows Franklin again living with his family headed by his father James Madison Carter, Jr. Included within the household where two of his cousins, the children of his uncle David Louis Carter, Mamie and Robert Carter. His grandmother Frances Coats Carter and her sister Catherine Coats were also included in the home. James Madison Carter, Jr.'s occupation was given as farmer.

Franklin Carter was drafted into the U.S. Army at Marlin, Texas on July 21, 1918. This was about a year after the death of his father on February 2, 1917. He was assigned to Company 'F' of the 45th Infantry. Franklin, or Frank as he had now become known, was discharged about six months later from the Army at Fort Gordon, GA on February 6, 1919. The peace treaty with Germany on November 21, 1918, had made his continuing service to his country unnecessary. Frank's discharge papers stated he was a farmer, had grey eyes, brown hair, dark complexion and stood 5 feet 7 inches high.

Franklin Eli Carter 1917

Following his return from the Army, Frank found himself in a home headed by his younger brother Obed J. Carter. The 1920 Texas, Limestone County census which was taken on February 13, 1920, shows Frank listed with his family. His occupation was given as farm laborer.

However, it appears Frank had more on his mind then farming. A pretty young lady had entered his life.

Frank Carter married Ruby Mae Johnson on March 13, 1920. The marriage license was issued from Burleson County, TX with the seal of office in Caldwell, TX. Ruby was born September 20, 1899, in Gilman, Ellis County, TX, the daughter of Marion Decalb Johnson and Leta Eola Williamson.

Ruby Mae Johnson and Franklin Eli Carter

Frank's first child, Sherwood Johnson Carter, was born in Big Hill, Limestone County, TX on March 16, 1921. His second child, James Milton Carter, was born in Mart, McLennan County, TX on June 6, 1924. While Mart, TX is located in McLennan County, the town borders Limestone County which was where the Carters and Rutherfords primarily lived but burying their deceased in the Mart Cemetery. Mart had to be the community close to where their families lived.

The family moved to McAdoo, Dickens County TX about the year 1925, where the family was found for the 1930 census. Frank's occupation at that time was 'trader, livestock'. There were two sons recorded, Sherwood and Milton. The family listing followed that of Ben Eldridge and his wife Ollie. The family moved to Hobbs, NM at about 1935, where Frank went to work for a water company supplying water to the various drillers working in the oil fields.

L to R, Obed Carter, Alice Carter Gibson, Cleo Carter Clampitt,
Shirley Carter Stevenson, Mamie Carter and Franklin Carter

Frank Carter was killed in an automobile accident near Pinon, Otero County, NM on November 11, 1961. He was buried at Memory Gardens Cemetery, Hobbs, NM. Frank's death certificate gave his occupation as "Manager Sinclair Gasoline Station." His address at the time of his death was 903 N. Coleman Ave., Hobbs, NM.

Truck Mishap Is Fatal to Frank Carter

Frank Carter, 67, of 903 North Coleman was fatally injured yesterday when his pickup truck crashed into a tree while he was on a deer hunting trip in the Sacramento Mountains. The accident happened three and a half miles west of Pinon, police said, on a dirt road.

Meagre reports from the area said Carter, alone in his Chevrolet pickup truck, was traveling the road when the vehicle struck a mud hole, causing him to lose control. The truck swerved from the road and struck a tree.

Carter left here Friday morning by himself to hunt deer. He told relatives that he planned to hunt in the Pinon area.

A resident of Hobbs since 1935, he was employed as an attendant at the Pecos Valley Oil Co. service station on the Carlsbad highway a few hundred yards west of the Marland, Broadway junction.

Survivors include his widow, Mrs. Ruby Carter; two sons, Milton Carter of Artesia, and Maj. Sherwood Carter, a member of the armed services stationed on Okinawa; and three sisters, Mrs. Frank Clampitt and Mrs. Johnny Gibson, both of Waco, Tex., and Mrs. Leroy Stevenson of Torrance, Calif.

An inquest was scheduled for last night in Artesia to determine the official cause of death. Funeral services still are pending, members of the family said.

Franklin Eli Carter Obituary

45

Ruby Johnson Carter married James B. Alexander in Hobbs in 1985. He later that same year passed away. Ruby Johnson Carter Alexander died on April 26, 1992. She was buried beside her first husband Frank E. Carter at the Memorial Gardens Cemetery in Hobbs, NM.

Franklin Eli Carter and Ruby Johnson Carter were the parents of two sons.

1. Sherwood Johnson Carter, Sr.
2. James Milton Carter

Sherwood Johnson Carter

Sherwood Johnson Carter was born at Big Hill, Limestone County, TX on March 1, 1921, the son of Franklin Eli Carter and Ruby Johnson Carter. Sherwood attended school in McAdoo, TX and worked in the fields with various crops. The family moved to Hobbs, NM at about 1935, where his father worked with the water company that supplied water to the oil fields.

Sherwood J. Carter married Nancy Margaret Speir at Sundown, TX on November 4, 1941. Nancy was born at Bogota, Red River County on March 20, 1922, the daughter of John Speir and Rose Parker Speir.

Sherwood became known at Nick, a popular dime novel mystery detective, during his military career. The Carter family served abroad on three different occasions. There was occupied Japan, the family traveled for two weeks by ocean steamer then Germany and finally Okinawa.

Sherwood Johnson Jr., Nancy Speir and Sherwood "Nick" Johnson Carter

Sherwood Johnson Carter circa 1944

Sherwood Johnson Carter circa 1954

Nick and Nancy were divorced in 1970. After retiring from the US Army as a Lt. Col, Nick worked for the Agency for International development in Viet Nam. He married Bernita Dykeman, a civil service secretary, while in Viet Nam. Nancy married William Kearney of Fort Lauderdale, FL in 1970. They divorced about 1980. Nancy moved back to NC.

Sherwood J. Carter and Nancy Speir Carter were the parents of four children.

L to R, Nancy Speir, Debra Delora, Donald Lane
and Richard Edward Carter

1. Sherwood Johnson Carter Jr.
2. Donald Lane Carter
3. Richard Edward Carter
4. Debra Delora Carter

Sherwood Johnson Carter Jr.

Sherwood Johnson Carter Jr. was born in Long Beach, Los Angeles County, CA on Jun 21, 1942, the son of Sherwood J. Carter Sr. and Nancy Speir Carter.

Sherwood graduated from the University of North Carolina for his undergraduate work and law degree. He served in the U.S. Army and did one tour in Viet Nam.

Sherwood married Patricia Ann Smith at Florence, Florence County, SC on December 23, 1966. They were later divorced, and he then married again to Bonnie ____, but they divorced. He then married Kristina Evelyn Lockaby Carter.

Sherwood passed away on March 3, 2019.

Donald Lane Carter

Donald Lane Carter was born in Lubbock, Lubbock County, TX on October 14, 1945, the son of Sherwood J. Carter Sr. and Nancy Speir Carter. Donald with his family moved from one military base to another during and after World War II, including Sendai, Tohoku Region and Honshu Island, Japan; Augsburg and Bad Tolz, Bavaria, Germany; Fort Campbell, Kentucky; Fort Bragg, NC; Fort Benning, GA and Sukiran, Okinawa. The family returned to Fayetteville, NC in 1963 where Donald graduated from Seventy-First High School.

Donald, or Don as he is also known, then attended East Carolina College in Greenville, NC. During his student days he worked as a lifeguard, construction worker and survey worker. It was also while attending East Carolina College he met and married fellow student Mary Elizabeth Bulluck. Mary, known as Beth, and Donald were married at Rocky Mount, Nash County, NC on August 19, 1967. Beth's parents were William R. Bulluck and Lula Mae Johnson of Rocky Mount, NC.

Donald Lane Carter Sr.

Mary Elizabeth Bulluck Carter

Following graduation in 1968, Don began his career as an Educator in the North Carolina Community College System where he instructed at three community colleges. He next taught in the Nash County Public Schools while working on his Master's Degree. He received his Master's Degree in Education from North Carolina State University. Later, he worked for the Governor's Office and then Director of the Evening Start Program with the N.C. Public Instruction from where he retired.

Beth last worked as a secretary at Dorothea Dix State Hospital for many years in Raleigh from where she retired in 2012. Don and Beth are the parents of two boys, Donald Lane Carter Jr. born in 1968 and William (Joey) Johnson Carter, born in 1971. Joey died at the age of 24 in 1996 of a brain stem tumor.

Donald Lane, Jr. and William Johnson Carter

1. Donald Lane Carter Jr.
2. William Johnson Carter

Donald Lane Carter Jr.

Donald Lane Carter Jr. was born in 1968, the son of Don and Beth Carter of Cary, NC. Known primarily as Lane, he graduated from Pembroke State University with a double major in Criminal Justice and History. Lane started his career with the North Carolina Department of Corrections, then moved to Probation and Parole and is now with the Department of Labor.

While a student at Pembroke Lane met and married Jolinda Swartout. They became the parent of two lovely girls; they were later divorced.

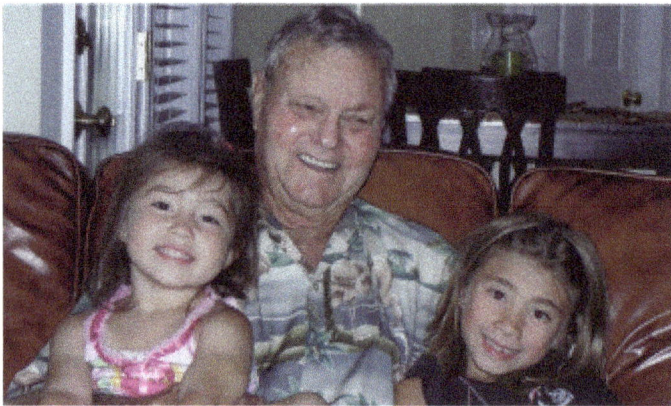

Lauren, Sherwood Johnson, Sr. and Kamiel Carter

Lauren and Kamiel Carter

1. Kamiel Carter
2. Lauren Carter

Richard Edward Carter Sr.

Richard Edward Carter Sr. was born at Fort Campbell, Christian County, KY on June 11, 1950, the son of Sherwood J. Carter Sr. and Nancy Speir Carter.

Richard married Sara Marlane Smith on June 20, 1969. Sara, known as Marty, was born February 13, 1951, the daughter of Hershel Smith and Eulaine Smith.

Richard served in the U. S. Army, doing a tour in Viet Nam. He worked for the Cumberland County Sheriff's Department in Fayetteville. N.C. before he moved the family to Arizona. In Arizona he worked for the Prison system.

Richard died suddenly of a heart attack on July 7, 1994, at Tucson, Pima County Arizona. His ashes were taken to Hobbs, NM where he was buried next to his paternal grandparents.

Richard was the parent of two children.

L to R, Richard Edward Jr., Richard Edward Sr., Samantha Ann and Sara Smith Carter circa 1986

1. Richard Edward Carter Jr.
2. Samantha Ann Carter

Richard Edward Carter Jr.

Richard Edward Carter Jr. was born January 18, 1971, the son of Richard E. Carter and Marty Smith Carter. After graduating high school in Tucson, AZ, he joined the US Army serving 3 years. Upon discharge, he returned to his family home. Two weeks later, his father passed away. Richard then went to work for the Arizona State Prison System. He became an expert in firearms training and served on the PERT team. Richard retired from the prison system and worked for the Diplomatic Security Service. Richard passed away on November 26, 2019.

Samantha Ann Carter

Samantha Ann Carter was born October 6, 1980, the daughter of Richard E. Carter and Marty Smith Carter. Samantha served in the US Army. She married Pablo Munevan in 2005; they were divorced in 2008. There was one child born of this marriage.

Samantha married Jhonnie Santiago Torres on March 20, 1012.

1. Sebastian Charlie Munevan, born March 25, 2006

Debra Delora Carter

Debra Delora Carter was born at Fort Campbell, Christian County, KY on September 4, 1952, the daughter of Sherwood J. Carter Sr. and Nancy Speir Carter. Debra graduated from Seventy-First High School in Fayetteville, NC. She married Ronald (Ron) James Jackson on November 7, 1969. Ron is the son of Charles James Jackson and Margaret Williams. Debra and Ron were divorced in 1977.

Debra graduated from Fayetteville Technical School in 1983 with an Associate's Degree in Nursing.

Following a year tour as a nurse in Saudi Arabia, Debra married Robert Davis McCloud on September 28, 1992, in Williamsburg, VA, City of Williamsburg County. Robert was born in Warrenton, VA on May 31, 1938, the son of James Edgar McCloud and Regina Robert Carder.

Robert Davis and Debra Delora Carter McCloud

Debra recently retired from the Veteran Hospital System after 30 some year of service. She is the parent of one child.

1. Veronika Ann Jackson

Veronika Ann Jackson

Veronika Ann Jackson was born at Fort Hood, TX on March 23, 1971, the daughter of Debra D. Carter and Ronald James Jackson. Veronika, known as Roni, attended school in the Cumberland County school system, graduating from Douglas Byrd High School in June 1989. Roni next attended the University of North Carolina at Charlotte, graduating in May 1993, with a degree in English.

Roni joined the U. S. Navy upon graduating. She was sent to Guam where she met and married Paul Schreck on December 3, 1995. Paul was an orthopedic corpsman and is a computer tech.

After returning to the states, Roni attended and graduated from Anne Arundel Community College as a Physician Assistant. Upon graduation, she took a commission and rejoined the Navy where she earned her Master's Degree. After ten years, she resigned her commission then began her career as a PA-C.

Roni and Paul divorced in 2005. She later married Corey Surber, a U. S. Marine Corps Warrant Officer on October 20, 2007. The family currently lives in Jacksonville, N.C. Roni is the parent of two lovely girls.

Veronika Ann Jackson Surber and Margaret Mae Schreck

Margaret Mae and Jacqualine Olivia Schreck

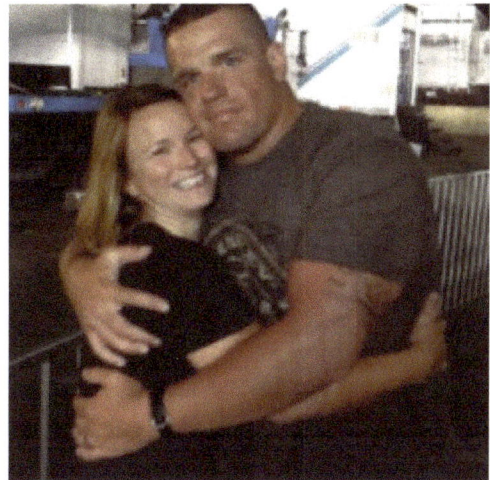

Veronika Ann Jackson and Corey Surber

1. Jacqualine Olivia Schreck, born July 6, 2001
2. Margaret Mae Schreck, born Nov. 11, 2004

James Milton Carter

James Milton Carter was born at Mart, TX on June 6, 1924, the son of Franklin Eli Carter and Ruby Johnson Carter. During WW II, Jim served in administration with the Army Air Corps.

James Milton Carter circa 1935

James, known as Jim or Milton, M. Carter married Doris Lee McCarthy on September 5, 1943. Doris was born on March 1, 1926, in Eliasville, Young County, TX, the daughter of Floyd Wm. McCarthy and Thelma Agatha Walker. The Walker family was located on the 1940 Texas, Stephen County census where Floyd was noted working as a 'pumper, oil company.' Floyd McCarthy was born in Dekalb County, IL, Thelma was born in Parker County, Texas.

Doris McCarthy and James Milton Carter circa 1943

James and Doris were the parents of four children, James Jr, Frances, Donna, and Roy. Doris died November 26, 1950, in Hobbs, NM. She was buried in Lovington Cemetery, Lea County, Lovington, NM.

James married Margorie Garnelle Thompson (Boyd) about 1952. Marge was previously married to Mr. John Vance Thompson and they had two sons, Charles Michael Thompson, born in Longview, Gregg County, TX and John Richard Thompson, born in Magnolia, Columbia County, AR. Mike and Johnnie later changed their last name to Carter while serving in the military. James and Marge were divorced in 1966.

James married Marion June Briggs on April 8, 1967. Marion, known as June, had been previously married to Lewis Ray Bradshaw and they had two sons Bobby Ray Bradshaw, born in Gaines County, TX and Stephen Lee Bradshaw born in McLennan, TX and a daughter Letha Shareen Bradshaw, born in Gains County, TX. Stephen was given the name of "Carter" at birth and was later adopted by James.

James worked for Texaco/Texas Oil Company as a "pumper/oil field" worker in oil fields around Buckeye, NM, Artesia, NM and finally Andrews, TX. While with Texaco, James worked his way up to Assistant Production Superintendent. He left Texaco after twenty years and went to work as a Production Superintendent with Aminoil in Kuwait. He worked with Aminoil for eight years. He then returned to the States where he and June lived in Alvin, TX while James worked for Clinton Oil Company in Houston for about two years as Production Superintendent.

James decided to go back overseas working for Petromer Trend in Papua, New Guinea. James, June and Stephen lived in Singapore for about two years while he commuted to New Guinea. They decided to move back to the States to Ruidosa, NM, while James still commuted to New Guinea for about another year and half. He last worked in the oil business for Meddars Oil Company in Wichita Falls, TX. He worked for Meddars for about six years as Drilling and Production Superintendent. James retired from the oil business in 1986 or 1987, then he, June and Stephen moved back to Ruidosa, NM.

James Milton Carter died in Ruidosa, NM on October 28, 2011. He was cremated and buried beside his first wife Doris in Lovington, NM. James was survived by his wife Marion June and seven children, James Carter Jr., Frances Evans, Charles Michael Carter, Donna Berry, John Richard Carter, Roy Carter and Stephen Lee Carter. He was also survived by twelve grandchildren and seventeen great grandchildren.

James Milton Carter was the parent of four children, one adopted child and two others.

L to R, Patty Carter, John "Johney" Richard Thompson Carter, Jerry Berry, Donna Lynn Carter Berry, Frances Elaine Carter Evans, Lloyd Evans, Jan Carter Charles "Mike" Michael Thompson Carter, Suzanne Carter and Roy William Carter

Peggy Sue and James Milton Carter Jr.

Dawn Carter and Bryan Mills

1. James Milton Carter Jr., November 1, 1944
2. Frances Elaine Carter, April 8, 1946
3. Donna Lynn Carter, August 10, 1947
4. Roy William Carter, June 25, 1950
5. Charles Michael Thompson Carter, September 28, 1946
6. John Richard Thompson Carter, June 6, 1948
7. Stephen Lee Bradshaw Carter, March 11, 1963

THE COATS FAMILY

Morgan Coats was born about 1802 in South Carolina; he died April 11, 1863, in Catahoula Parish, Louisiana. He is believed to have married Sophia Rawlings from North Carolina about 1824.

Children:

1. George Washington Coats, born May 15, 1825, GA; died Aug. 25, 1889, Leon Co., TX
2. William J. (Billy) Coats, born1818, GA, died Dec. 16, 1898, Keechi, Leon Co. TX
3. Harriet Coats, born 1831 GA
4. John Coats, born 1832 CA, died 1864, LA
5. Catherine (Taffie) Coats, born 1834, GA, died March 15, 1915, McLennan Co., TX
6. Frances Ann Coats, born Sept. 1838, Lauderdale Co., MS, died Jan. 1914, Waco, McLennan, TX

The family was found attending Baptist Church in Lauderdale Co., MS on April 1838. Morgan Coats paid taxes in Lauderdale County in 1840.

On 21 Oct 1846: John P. Ogden and his wife Susan Frances Parham to Morgan Coats & Allen Nix Trustees of the First Baptist Church for the benefit and use of the Baptist Church on Little River. (One Acre)

Sophia Coats died of cholera in August 1850; according to the1850 Mortality Schedule, therefore she was not listed with the family for the 1850 Catahoula Parish, LA census which was taken on August 20, 1850.

The 1850 census:

1. Morgan Coats, age 48, Planter, born SC
2. George Coats, age 25, born GA
3. Wm. Coats, age 22, born GA
4. Harriet Coats, age 19, born GA
5. John Coats, age 18, born GA
6. Catherine Coats, age 16, born GA
7. Frances Coats, age 12, born Miss

George Coats

George W. Coats, a 45-year-old farmer from Georgia was married to Martha Coats, a 26 year old woman from Louisiana, living in Trinity, Catahoula Parish, for the 1870 census. There was one child named Elijah Coats, age 3/12. There was $1250 of real estate property value and $800 of personal property recorded. It appears he inherited his father's estate.

The George Coats family was found on the 1880 Texas census, Leon County living very near to his sister Frances Ann Coats Carter. George's wife, 36-year-old Martha C. Coats, was born in Louisiana. There were two children in the home, Elijah B. Coats, age 10 and John T. Coats, age 7. Both children had been born in Louisiana. Included in the household was Catherine Coats, age 40, who was also born in Louisiana.

There is a photograph in the Carter Family collection showing six men standing with shotguns in their hands in what appears to have been a hunting camp. Two of these men are identified as Elijah Coats and George Coats. Their ages appear to be close enough to be father and son, but more likely brothers or cousins.

Children from the 1880 census,

1. Elijah B. Coats, born 1870
2. John T. Coats, born 1873

Catherine Coats

Catherine Coats was born in Georgia about the year 1834. Catherine, France's spinster sister, has been used to identify various family members on census because she seems to have floated from family to family. She was still living in Catahoula Parish, LA in 1870 where she was found within the family of her brother W. J. Coats. Coats was married to Martha Coats, age 28 years and there were two children, Mary Coats, age 10 and a brother Thomas Coats, age 1 years.

The first family Catherine Coats was listed with on census in Texas was in 1880, when she was found within the George W. Coats family in Leon County, Texas.

The 1900 Texas census, Limestone County locates Catherine living within the Dave (David) L. Carter family. She was noted as Dave's aunt and recorded a birth date of September 1836 in Georgia. She listed her parents as both having been born in South Carolina.

For the 1910 Texas census Catherine was found in the home of James M. Carter Jr. in McLennan County. Catherine's sister Frances Coats Carter, James' mother, was also in the household. Catherine is believed to have passed away on March 15, 1915, McLennan County, Texas.

Frances Ann Coats

Frances Ann Coats was born in Mississippi in 1840. Frances Ann Coats married James M. Carter on May 29, 1860, at the Locus Grove (Baptist) on Little River, Catahoula Parish, Louisiana, see page 23.

THE RUTHERFORD FAMILY

The Rutherford surname is frequently noted as originating from the Scottish Lowlands and Northern Ireland. The family was part of the faction of families commonly referred to as Reivers or Border Bandits. The border between Scotland and England was a no man's land, so bad was the fighting between families a bishop of the church read a curse against them all from the pulpit in the Carlisle Cathedral.

The Rutherford Family

David Carter Sr. served under Gen. Griffith Rutherford in June 1779; this force gathered in North Carolina eventually joining the American Army of Gen Horatio Gates. A battle of American forces against the British led to the American defeat at Camden, South Carolina in August 1780 where Gen. Rutherford and David Carter were both captured.

There are counties of Rutherford in both NC and TN. There is also a town of Rutherfordton in NC. There was also a U.S. president named Rutherford B. Hayes. So, the name is associated with the early history of America.

Lindsey J. Rutherford

Lindsey J. Rutherford was born in 1805 in Tennessee. He married Hettie Hodges, who was born in 1815 in Tennessee. Research from an unknown source claims there were 10 children from the marriage. What is known about the family is that Lindsey Rutherford married Hettie Hodges in Hardeman, TN in September 1830. Hardeman, TN is in west Tennessee adjacent the Mississippi border.

The 1850 Mississippi census, District 6, Itawamba shows the Lindsey Rutherford family with a listing of seven Rutherford family children recorded below. The 1860 Texas census, Jasper County shows this family under the name of L.G. Rutherford, who was a fifty-year-old farmer. There were two additional children, items 8 and 9 below, in the family listing seen below.

The 1870 Texas census, Leon County locates the family of L.G. Rutherford listed just below the family of J.E. Rutherford, who apparently was Lindsey's son James E. Rutherford. There was an additional child listed who did not appear on the 1860 census, his name was Jacob Rutherford, age 15, born in MS.

The 1880 Texas census, Limestone County, finds L.J. and H. H. Rutherford living within the home of S. L. (Shelton Lindsey) and J. P. (Josephine Powell) Rutherford.

1. James Edward Rutherford, age 15, born in TN
2. Jasper G. Rutherford, age 13, born in AR
3. Rebecca A. Rutherford, age 11. born in AR
4. Martha J. Rutherford, age 9, born in AK
5. Shelton Lindsey Rutherford, age 5, born AK
6. Able David Rutherford, age 2, born TN
7. Mary L. Rutherford, age 6/12, born MS
8. Jacob Rutherford, then age 18, born MS
9. Parthenia Rutherford, then age 8, born in MS
10. Elizabeth Ann Rutherford, then age 3, born in TX

James Edward Rutherford

James Edward Rutherford was born in Tennessee in 1835 the son of Lindsey J. Rutherford and Hettie Hodges. He married Martha Ann Rogers, time and place unknown, she was born in 1837 in Alabama.

The family was found for the 1900 Texas, Limestone County census under the name of Jim Rutherford. Children listed in the home were Shade L. Rutherford, David D. Rutherford and Hettie E. Rutherford Crockett. Hettie's husband Andy Crockett and one child, Ida Crockett, were also listed as was a William L. Crockett, relationship uncertain.

Martha died about 1900 in Freestone County, TX. James died in 1908 in Buna, Jasper County, TX.

There were seven known children of this family.

1. Isaac N. Rutherford, born 1860
2. Mary Angeline Rutherford, born 1865
3. Shelton Lee Rutherford
4. Hettie E. Rutherford
5. Lindsey Shade Rutherford
6. David D. or A. Rutherford, born October 1876
7. O'Leatha Rutherford, not on 1900 home census

Shelton Lee Rutherford

Shelton Lee Rutherford was born on December 8, 1866, the son of James E. Rutherford and Martha Ann Rogers. Shelton married Lillie Rosetta Yerby, she was born May 30, 1876.

Shelton Lee Rutherford and Lillie Rosetta Yerby Rutherford are both buried in Mart, Texas cemetery. She died December 14, 1926, he died January 24, 1928.

Shelton Lee Rutherford had four children; order of birth uncertain.

1. John David Rutherford
2. Oma Rutherford
3. Samuel Lee Rutherford
4. Callie Rutherford

Hettie E. Rutherford

Hettie E. Rutherford was born in Texas in January 1870, the daughter of James E. Rutherford and Martha Ann Rogers. Hettie married Andy Crockett, probably in Limestone County about 1891. This family was listed with her parents for the 1900 Texas, Limestone County census. There was one child listed at that time, Ida V. Crockett.

1. Ida V. Crockett, born Nov. 1893
2. W. Corbett Crockett

Shelton Lindsey Rutherford

Shelton Lindsey Rutherford was born in Mississippi in June 18, 1845, the son of Lindsey J. Rutherford and Hettie Hodges. Shelton married Josephine Powell on August 18, 1868, in Leon County, TX. She was born in 1848 in Tennessee. Her parents were both born in South Carolina. The family was living in Kosse J. Precinct # 5, Limestone County, Texas for the 1880 census, there were five children listed in the family, all daughters. Also listed in the family was Shelton's parents L.J. Rutherford and H. Rutherford.

The 1900 Texas census, Justice Precinct 2, Bell County shows this family with two additional children, items 6 and 7 added below. Callie Rutherford Phillips, her husband William E. Phillips and one child named Ruby Pearl Phillips were also in the family listing.

The family was found in Justice Precinct 2, Limestone County, for the 1910 Texas census. A grandson name Barney E. Rutherford and a servant were the only family members listed. The 1920 Limestone County, Justice Precinct # 8 shows the family listed on the census just after the children of their daughter Olivia Ashabranner and the children of their daughter Irene Rutherford Carter. Recorded in the home was a 15-year-old grandson Edgar Rutherford.

S. L. Rutherford died in Waco, McLennan County, TX on June 12, 1926, he was buried in the Mart Cemetery, Mart, Texas. This information comes from an application for Civil War Confederate Pension from Mrs. J. H. Rutherford, signed on June 28, 1926, in Waco, TX. Sadly,

Josephine Powell Rutherford did not get a chance to enjoy any of her husband's pension because she passed away on July 21, 1926.

1. (L.D)Dora Rutherford, age 10 (Not found on 1900 census)
2. S. B. Rutherford, age 8
3. J. G. Rutherford, age 6 (should be Mattie Eugenia Irene Rutherford, J. could be an I)
4. Lula Rutherford, age 4 (Not found on 1900 census)
5. Callie Rutherford, age 3/12
6. Oliva Rutherford, age 18, birth year 1881
7. Jasper M. Rutherford, age 16, birth year 1883

Mattie Eugenia Irene Rutherford

Mattie Eugenia Irene Rutherford was born in Llano, Llano County, TX on June 8, 1874, the daughter of Shelton Lindsey Rutherford and Josephine Powell. Mattie, known as Rene, married James Madison Carter, Jr. See Section II, page 31.

Callie Rutherford

Callie Rutherford was born in Texas in 1880, the daughter of Shelton Lindsay Rutherford and Josephine Powell. Callie was married to William E. Phillips; he was born in 1877. There was one known child of this marriage.

1. Ruby Pearl Phillips

Olivia Rutherford

Olivia Rutherford was born in Texas in 1882, the daughter of Shelton Lindsey Rutherford and Josephine Powell. Olivia married Carl Ashabranner about 1904, probably in Limestone County. The family was found on the 1920 Texas, Limestone County census, Justice Precinct # 8, living on Big Hill Road and listed between Olivia's sister Irene Carter and her father Shelton Rutherford. There were six children recorded in the home at that time. Their names are listed below.

At the time Irene Rutherford Carter died in September 1948, an obituary noted Olivia Ashabranner was the sole surviving Rutherford sibling; she was then living in Waco, Texas.

1. Thelma Ashabranner, age 15
2. Birnice Ashabranner, age 14
3. Alpha Ashabranner (m) age 10
4. Bertha Ashabranner, age 7
5. Burr Ashabranner (m) age 4 &11/12
6. Etha Ashabranner, age 2 & 7/12

David A. Rutherford

David A. Rutherford was born about the year 1849, the son of Lindsey J. Rutherford and Hettie Hodges. David married M. Laurissa Day. There appears to be three children of this marriage.

1. Florence Rutherford
2. Lloyd Rutherford
3. Maude Ann Rutherford, see Benjamin Franklin Carter, page 39.

THE JOHNSON FAMILY

The delineation of these Johnson family members has been greatly assisted by three Family Record pages from an old family bible. Who originally owned the bible and where these two pages came from is not known by this researcher. What is certain though is these pages carry the birth information for three family generations. Using these three pages and the 1850 Mississippi census, Oktibbeha County, members of this family to 1850 can be identified. The parents on the Family Record pages were identified as L. Johnson, born July 24, 1805 and Elzary (Johnson), born September 30, 1815. Using the 1850 census L. Johnson was identified as Lenard Johnson, a brick mason from North Carolina and his wife Elzira Johnson who was recorded as born in Alabama.

The children listed below follow what was recorded in the family record section then compared to what the 1850 census records show.

1. W. J. Johnson, born June 5the, 1836 (William Johnson) born in Tenn
2. J. H. Johnson, born Febu. 19th, 1838 (John Johnson) born in Miss
3. L.S. Johnson, born Octob 19th. 1839 (Lenard Johnson) born in Ala
4. M. An P. (Johnson), born Nov. 11th 1841 (Margaret Johnson) do, died Jan. 12, 1858
5. J. Pinkney (Johnson), born Nov. 1th, 1843 (James Johnson) do, died July 25, 1863
6. M.E. L.Lan (Johnson), born Dec. 23th, 1846 (Malinda Johnson) Miss
7. A. Hutson (Johnson), born Octo 1th 1849 (Andrew Johnson) do

The Family Record pages shows the birth of three additional children, G. Perry (Johnson) born March 23, 1851; M. Matilda (Johnson) born March 22, 1853, and S. Marilda (Johnson) born April 2, 1860.

The 1860 Mississippi census, Township 20, Choctaw, listed the parents as Lenard Johnson, age 50 and Eliza Johnson, age 48 and the following children, William J. Johnson, Lenard S. Johnson, John Johnson, James Johnson, Elvira Johnson and Malissa Johnson (age 6).

The Family Record pages records that Elzary Johnson died December 8, 1865, the place of death was not recorded. It appears the book holding the Family Records was passed to the oldest son William J. Johnson. No record of the death of Lenard Johnson was made.

William Jackson Johnson

The next family recorded in the Family Record pages was the family of William Jackson Johnson. The first family member listed was M. J. Johnson, borne(sic) April 9, 1843. This would have been William's wife Morning Tennessee Wimpy. The following children were recorded:

1. Arminda Johnson, born May 7, 1868
2. Lavisa Johnson, born Dec. 31st, 1870
3. Marion Decalb (Johnson), born Nov. 9th, 1873
4. Dewitty Johnson, born May 13th, 1876
5. Netty Johnson, born on May 13th, 1878
6. Cora Johnson, born Sept 19th, 1880

Morning Tennessee (known as Tenny) Wimpy was born in Mississippi on April 9, 1843, the daughter of David R. Wimpy and Mary S. Rodgers. The Wimpy family was found for the 1850 Mississippi census living in Southern Division, Tishomingo County. There were three children in the family at that time, Susan S. Wimpy, Mourning T. Wimpy and Francis B. Wimpy. The oldest child was born in Alabama while the last two were born in Mississippi. David was a farmer from South Carolina, his wife was born in Alabama, there was Real Estate valued as $225.00 recorded.

The 1860 Mississippi census, Tishomingo County locates Tennessee Wimpy living in the home of George P. Roland and his wife Mary Roland, there were seven young children in this family. Tenny's relationship to this family was not given. It is believed Tenny was married during the Civil War to a Mr. Baxter who did not survive the war. Tenny married William Jackson Johnson on her birthday April 9, 1865.

The Johnson family was found on the 1870 Mississippi census, Choctaw County, Township 21, Range 11 show William and his wife Tennessee M., age 24- and 2-year-old Arminda. William was a wood workman. The family listed following William on the census was Andrew H. Johnson, age 21, and also a wood workman.

Arminda Johnson was born May 7, 1868. She died on November 26, 1876, as the result of burns she received when jumping over an open fire her dress caught on fire. Her mother received severe burns on her hands in an attempt to put the fire out.

The 1880 Mississippi census, Sumner County list the Johnson family, there were by this time four additional children added to the family, Lovisa, age 9, Marvin, age 6, Willis, age 4, and Nettie Johnson, age 2. This census is very difficult to read, but as best can be read William's occupation was given as Gen. Artist, whatever that means.

William J. Johnson died on August 1, 1881, of typhoid fever, said to have been complicated be, because of the effect of having been a prisoner of war during the Civil War. A 6th child, Cora Johnson, born on Sept. 19, 1880 was added to the family.

Morning T. Wimpy Johnson married F. A. Evans on November 29, 1887. He died on February 19, 1900. Morning Johnson Evans died Wednesday at 8:35 pm on January 22, 1919, in Montgomery County, Alabama. She was buried in Huntsville, Madison County, Alabama.

There was another family recorded on the Family Record pages. This would be the family of Lavisa Johnson who married A. C. Gammill. His date of birth was Jan 27, 1860.

1. Nancy Ora Gammill, born Oct. 5, 1890, (died Nov. 26, 1899)
2. Leslie Gammill, born July 15, 1892, (died July 30, 1898)
3. Homer Gammill, born Oct. 18, 1894
4. Nettie Gammill, born Sept. 15, 1898
5. Cappie Gammill, born Aug. 2, 1903

There was one last birth entry in the sheets of the Family Records, this was for Lottie Sanders born Dec. 8, 1897. The book housing the Family Records apparently was passed to the Gammill Family. The last entry recorded in the death section of the book was "Our Darling Mother Mrs. M. T. Evans died Jan. 22. 1919 Wednesday 8:35 pm."

Marion Decalb Johnson

Marion Decalb Johnson was born November 9, 1873, in Jackson, Hines County, Mississippi the son of William J. Johnson and Morning Tennessee Wimpy. Marion married Leta Eola Williamson on June 30, 1895, at Oliver School House, Texas. Leta was born February 17, 1878, at Harpersville, Shelby County, Alabama the daughter of James Williamson and Alice Woodly Beville.

L to R, Cora Johnson, Marion Decalb Johnson and Morning Tennessee (Johnson) Wimpy

The Johnson family was living in Upshur County, TX for the 1900 census where Marion was working as a "Sawmill Forman." Nearly all the employed people listed on this page of the census were sawmill workers. There were three children in the home all born in Texas, Eula, Willie and Rubie. The family lost a child when Mamie Inez Johnson was born on March 27, 1907 then passing away on April 20, 1907.

For the 1910 Oklahoma census, Webbers Falls, Muskogee County shows Marion working as a house carpenter. There were six children listed in the home, Eula Lee Johnson, age 13, William J. Johnson, age 12, Ruby M. Johnson, age 10, Marion D. Johnson, age 8, Mary G. Johnson, age 7 and Veloy Glenn Johnson, age 1. By the year 1913, the family was living in Limestone County, TX.

The 1920 Texas census, Trinity County, Precinct #2 finds the Johnson family, Marion was working as a laborer carpenter. There were nine children in the home, Eula Lee Johnson, the oldest, was not listed. Marion D. Johnson died on May 9, 1923, at Spur, Dickens County, TX.

He was buried at Girard Cemetery, Girard, Kent County, TX. Marion died as the result of a ruptured appendix. His family was allowed into the operating room during surgery. Marion was a farmer and a carpenter.

Leta later married Will Hitt and still later she married Steve Jarvis on November 17, 1934. Leta died on April 16, 1962, at Hobbs, NM. She was buried in Prairie View Cemetery, in Hobbs NM. Marion Decalb Johnson and Leta Eola Williamson were the parents of twelve known children. It appears the Family Records book or Bible was passed into the hands of the Melvin Roy Johnson family.

1. Eula Lee Johnson
2. James William Johnson
3. Ruby Mae Johnson
4. Marion Dennis Johnson
5. Mary Gladys Johnson
6. Mamie Inez Johnson, born March 27, 1907, died April 20, 1907
7. Glyn Veloy Johnson
8. Melvin Roy Johnson
9. Maggie Alice Johnson
10. Tennessee Louise Johnson
11. Little Brother Johnson, born July 18, 1918, died July 22, 1918
12. Eugene Laverne Johnson, born Sept. 7, 1919, died Dec. 30, 1920

Eula Lee Johnson

Eula Lee Johnson was born at Mart, TX on September 13, 1896, the daughter of Marion Decalb Johnson and Leta Williamson Johnson. Eula married Andrew Washington Martin on April 8, 1917. Andrew, known as Andy, was born in Gustine, Comanche County, TX on September 16, 1892, the son of Lee Andrew Martin and Sally Catherine Johnson.

Andrew W. Martin died in an automobile accident on May 28, 1966 or 1967, in Gustine, Comanche County, TX. He was buried in Hobbs, NM. Eula Lee Johnson Martin died July 9, 1974. She was buried in Hobbs, NM. There were three known children.

1. Marion Lee Martin
2. Murray Carlysle Martin, born June 24, 1924, Mart, Limestone County, TX
3. Nita Ruth Martin

James William Johnson

James William Johnson was born in Texas on December 8, 1897, the son of Marion Decalb Johnson and Leta Williamson Johnson. James, known as Willy, married Lula Mae Little in Mart, TX on January 5, 1927. Lula Mae Little was born December 12, 1907, in Mart, TX, the daughter of James Walter Little and Dona Blankenship.

Lula Mae Little Johnson died of tuberculosis on March 7, 1937. She was buried in Plainview Memorial Park, Plainview, Hale County, TX. James later married Pearl Seagal in 1945 in Borger, TX.

James William Johnson died in Lubbock, Lubbock County, TX in Feb. 1982. There were three known children of this family.

1. Billie Mae Johnson
2. James William Johnson, Jr.
3. Franklin D. Johnson

Ruby Mae Johnson

Ruby Mae Johnson was born on September 20, 1899, at Gilman, Ellis County, TX, the daughter of Marion Decalb Johnson and Leta Williamson Johnson. Ruby Mae married Franklin Eli Carter on March 13, 1920, at Burleson County, TX. See page 43.

Marion Dennis Johnson

Marion Dennis Johnson was born in Mississippi on April 22, 1902, the son of Marion Declab Johnson and Leta Williamson Johnson. Marion married Effie Ruth Frazier in 1924. He married Jessie Roberson in 1942.

Mary Gladys Johnson

Mary Gladys Johnson was born in Mississippi on April 23, 1904, the daughter of Marion Decalb Johnson and Leta Williamson Johnson. Mary married Neal (Neil) Benjamin Hardee on January 14, 1925. Neal died on February 7, 1934. Mary later married Norman Agusta Sikes on March 28, 1939.

Neal Durwood Hardee was born on October 25, 1925. He died in an airplane crash in China on October 30, 1945. He was buried beside his father Neal B. Hardee in an Ira, TX cemetery.

Glyn Veloy Johnson

Glyn Veloy Johnson was born in Oklahoma on May 17, 1908, the son of Marion Decalb Johnson and Leta Williamson Johnson. Glyn married Lorna Powers on January 20, 1934.

Glyn died on May 23, 1949.

Melvin Roy Johnson

Melvin Roy Johnson was born August 16, 1910, the son of Marion Decalb Johnson and Leta Williamson Johnson. Melvin married Leona Clark on May 24, 1930.

Maggie Alice Johnson

Maggie Alice Johnson was born April 12, 1913, the daughter of Marion Decalb Johnson and Leta Williamson Johnson. Maggie married L.C. Byrd on September 28, 1928. She married Earl Cathcart in 1942. She married Rolla Lawrence Gracey on October 2, 1946. She is the parent of one known child.

1. Harold Dean Byrd died on August 30, 1946.

Tennessee Louise Johnson

Tennessee Louise Johnson was born September 2, 1915, the daughter of Marion Decalb Johnson and Leta Williamson. Tennessee married William Luther Hollingsworth on October 8, 1933. She married David Emory Horstman on June 24, 1946. She married _____ on June 23, 1951.

DeWitty Johnson

DeWitty Johnson was born May 13, 1876, the daughter of William J. Johnson and Morning Wimpy Johnson. She married J. A. Sanders on September 2, 1897.

Netty Johnson

Netty Johnson was born May 13, 1878, the daughter of William J. Johnson and Morning Wimpy Johnson. Netty married J. L. Sanders on December 9, 1894. They had a daughter Lottie Sanders. She was the last name recorded in the birth section of the Family Records.

Cora Johnson

Cora Johnson was born September 19, 1880, the daughter of William Jackson Johnson and Morning Wimpy Johnson. Cora never married. She became a nurse in Corinth, Mississippi.

THE WILLIAMSON FAMILY

The Williamson family has been a challenge to research as important events took place during the interval of time between the 1880 census and the 1900 census when little was recorded.

J. Williamson, age 22 farmer born in Alabama, was found on the 1880 Alabama census, Broken Arrow and Cropwell, St Clair County. Twenty-one-year-old Alaice(sic) Williamson was recorded as wife with two children, Leta Williamson, age 2 and Ella Williamson, age 1. There was a 24-year-old William Williamson who was probably a brother to J. J. Williamson was probably James Williamson whose mother and father were noted as born in Alabama.

A family story relates Alice Wodley Beville (Williamson) "While moving to Texas in a covered Wagon with her husband James Williamson and three daughters (Leta, the oldest being 5 years of age) her husband died of pneumonia. After burial, she continued on with her daughters in the covered wagon. She weighed 98 pounds."

It appears the widow Alice W. Beville Williamson remarried to William Lee Wolverton. The 1910 Texas, Limestone County, TX census show this family, they had been married 25 years which means they were married in 1885 probably just as she reached Texas. Her daughter Leta was married to Marion D. Johnson on June 30, 1895, at the Oliver School House, Texas.

There were three children, all girls, born of the Williamson relationship, there appears to have been three more children with the Wolverton marriage. There was another child in the home, a Lora L. Wolverton, age 7 years for the 1910 census, relationship uncertain.

1. Leta Eola Williamson
2. Ella Williamson
3. Maggie Williamson
4. Mamie Wolverton
5. John Grover Wolverton
6. Myrtle Wolverton

Ella Williamson married James Otis Wilson, three children, Vera Wilson married to a Mr. Alexander, Clinton Wilson, James Otis Wilson.

Maggie Williamson married to Mr. Mixon, three children, Treva Inex Mixon married Mr. Weatherspoon; Mary Alice Mixon married Mr. Bledsoe and James D. Mixon.

1 RUBY MAY JOHNSON CARTER	13 TREVA ENEZ MIXON WITHERSPOON	
2 MYRTLE WOLVERTON DOUGAS	14 LEE WOLVERTON	25 MARY ALICE MIXON BLEDSOE
3 EULA LEE JOHNSON MARTIN	15 HORA LEE WOLVERTON UNDERWOOD	26 JAMES OTIS WILSON
4 JAMES WILLIAM JOHNSON	16 JOHN GROVER WOLVERTON JR	
5 JAMES D. MIXON	17 MAGGIE ALICE JOHNSON GRACEY ★	
6 MAGGIE WILLIAMSON MIXON	18 CORETA SADLER MANN	
7 CLINTON WILSON	19 MARION DENNIS JOHNSON ★	
8 ELLA WILLIAMSON WILSON	20 MARY GLADYS JOHNSON HARDEE SIKES ★	
9 JOHN GROVER WOLVERTON	21 GLYN VALOY JOHNSON ★	
10 OLLIE CHRISTIE WOLVERTON	22 MELVIN ROB JOHNSON ★	
11 LETA BOLA WILLIAMSON JOHNSON	23 VERA WILSON ALEXANDER	
12 MAMIE WOLVERTON SADLER	24 ALICE BEVILL WILLIAMSON WOLVERTON	

THE SPEIR FAMILY

Much of the information contained in this write up about the Speir family comes from the research material of Gerald Lee King in his biographical compilation about the Speir family compiled for the 1986 publication entitled the "The Red River Recollection." Gerald L. King was the son of Cora Speir King; he was an attorney at Spring, Texas. His research effort was made during the 1980s, a very useful effort.

Francis M. Speir

Francis M. Speir was born in Georgia in 1846, the son of Hiram L. Speir and Jane Speir. The Hiram L. Spin(sic) family was located in Union Township, Iron County, Missouri for the 1860 Federal census. Hiram's age at that time was 47 years, born in Tennessee. His wife Jane was 43 years of age born in Alabama; there were six children in the household, William E., age 16, born in Georgia, Francis M. age 14 years, born in Georgia, Hiram E., age 12 born in Alabama, James S., age 10, born in Alabama, George W., age 8, born in Missouri, Thomas J., age 5, born in Missouri. Also found in the family listing was John Lane, age 22 years born in Tennessee and Martha M. Lane, age 17, born in Georgia. At this enumeration Hiram Speir listed a real estate value of $1,000.00 and a personal property value of $600.00. The two Lane children in the home were probably the children of John and Hepsey Lane. The Post Office was located at Polks Spring.

John Lane and his wife Hepsey Lane were both born in Tennessee, John in 1809, his wife about five years later about 1815. The family was found for the 1850 U. S. census living in District 76, Reynolds, Missouri, there were seven children in the family at that time, Matilda Lane, age 17; Robert Lane, age 14; John Lane, age 13 all born in Tennessee. The other four children Jasper Lane, age 7; Henry Lane, age 5; Martha Lane, age 2 and Mary Lane 0 were born in Missouri. This means the family moved to Missouri about the year 1853. John Lane was a farmer with a personal property value of $400.00.

The 1860 census locates the Lane family living in Union, Iron County, Missouri, John was a 52 year farmer while his wife was 40 years old. There were five children in the home at that time, Jasper Lane, age 17, Henry Lane, age 16, Martha Lane age 13, Mary Lane, age 10 and the additional member Elizabeth Lane, age 7 years. John Lane by this time had acquired $1,600 real estate property and $400 of personal property. The Post Office address for the family was Polks Spring.

The 1870 census locates the Lane family living in St. Francis Township in Wayne County, Missouri with a Post office located at Greenville, MO. John Layne(sic) was a 65-year-old farmer with $250 real estate value and $300 personal property value. Sixty-year-old Mary Lane was noted as 'keeping house'. There were two children in the home at that time, Martha, age 20 and Elizabeth, age 18.

The family listing directly after John Lane was the family of Frank Speer(sic), age 25 years and his wife Mary Lane Speer(sic), age 22. Frank Speer had $700.00 real estate value and $400 personal property. Missouri marriage records state Francis M. Spears(sic) married Mary Lane at Carter, Missouri on November 22, 1868. Francis was also recorded as Frank Speers(sic). Mary M. Lane was born April 2, 1850, in Missouri, the daughter of John Lane and Hepsey Lane.

Family information states the Speir family was living in Gainesville, Cooke County, TX in 1879. However, efforts to locate the Speir family on any 1880 census have proven to be futile. It is believed Francis Speir died in 1888, probably in Cove, Polk County, Arkansas.

On the twentieth day of April 1892, Mary M. Speir(sic) "widow of Frances M. Speir deceased" at the Register of the Land Office at Camden Arkansas was given a tract of land containing 160 acres. The survey remarks are included here; The Land Grant to Mary M. Speir dated "twentieth day of April 1892" containing 160 acres. Property location described as:

"North West quarter of the North West quarter of Section twenty seven and the East half of the North East quarter and the North East quarter of the South East quarter of Section twenty eight in Township three South of Range thirty one West of the Fifth Principal Meridian in Arkansas"

This tract of land appears to have been located in the western part of Polk County, Arkansas very near the Tucker 160 acres homestead tract. On July 2, 1895, Mary sold the 160 acres she had received in the 1892 grant to G. M. Craig for $320.00. (Polk County, Arkansas deed book I, page 468)

The 1900 census locates this family registered in Township 2, Chickasaw Nation, Indian Territory. Three of her sons were living with her at the time, John Clayton Speir, age 18, James Y. Speir, age 16 and George C. Speir, age 5.

Mary Speir was located on the 1910 Garvin County, Oklahoma census living within the home of her son-in-law Clenton(sic) L. Cheatwood. They were living in the Elmore Township at Foster Village. Cheatwood's wife was misidentified as Preston Cheatwood, a twelve-year-old son named Charles M. Cheatwood made up the family listing. The only known daughter of Mary Speir was recorded as Belle Speir.

Mrs. Mary Speir died January 31, 1931, at the home of her son G. C. Speir near Martin, Texas at Clarendon, Donley County Texas. From an article that appeared in *The Clarendon News*, date February 5, 1931, under the heading of 'Grandmother Speir Buried Here Sunday' offered a few comments about her life. Since the age of eighteen Mary had been a member of the Missionary Baptist Church. A faith "in which she labored faithfully until she was prevented in her work by the encroachment of advancing years." At the time of her death, Mary was survived by five sons; G. C. Speir, T. J. Speir, J. Y. Speir all living near Clarendon, Texas; J. C. Speir living at Hayden, OK and W. B. Speir living at Bogata, Texas.

The death certificate for Mary Speir was signed by her son T. J. Speir of Clarendon. Burial was in the Citizens Cemetery the Undertaker was P.A. Buntin & Son. Interestingly, the name of Mary's parent could not be remembered as the question's answers were put down as "Don't know."

Francis (Frank) M. Speir and Mary Lane Speir were the parents of eleven known children. Six of the children are known.

1. William Baker Speir
2. Belle Speir
3. Thomas Jefferson Speir
4. John Clayton Speir, age 18
5. James Yancey Speir, age 16 for 1900 census, brn 9 April 1884, Cove Polk County Arkansas
6. George Carroll Speir, age 5 years for 1900 census

William Baker Speir

William Baker Speir was born August 20, 1872, at Iron County, MO, the eldest son of Francis (Frank) Speir and Mary M. Lane. William moved with his family to Gainesville, Cooke County, Texas in 1879. In 1883, William moved with his family to Cove, Polk County, Arkansas. Here he met and married Cora Etta Lee Tucker on February 28, 1892. Cora was born October 5, 1868, in Magnolia, Columbia County, Arkansas the daughter of William Henry Tucker and Millie Ann Smith. Her father was homesteading a tract of land near the Speir tract. William worked at a sawmill during this time

William Henry Tucker was born in Georgia on May 17, 1836. He served during the Civil War with Adams Reg., Ark. Inf. and Co. 'B', 27th Reg. Reg. Ark. Inf. Mr. Tucker was a Mason, a blacksmith and justice of the Peace in Cove, Polk county, Ark. Millie Ann Smith was born in Georgia in 1844. She died young.

The Speir family moved to Indian Territory in 1893 (the territory later becoming Oklahoma in 1907), then to Rosalie, TX at about 1895 where William purchased a tract of land. The 1900 Texas census locates this family in Precinct # 2 in Red River County, TX. There were three children in the family at the time which proved to be quite telling. The children were Grover, born Jan. 1893 in Arkansas; Mary M. L. born in November 1895, in Indian (Terr.) and John, born April 1898 in Texas. This notice about the children's places of birth not only proves the family moved frequently but was living in Indian Territory in 1895. William's occupation was noted as Blacksmith.

William operated a blacksmith shop in Rosalie, Texas. In 1910, he later built a blacksmith shop and garage in Bogata, Red River County, Texas which was then called the Bogata Blacksmith Shop. The 1910 Texas census noted the family living in Red River County; there were six children in the family at that time; Grover L.; Mary M. L.; John; Ethel, Jack and Cora. The 1920 Texas census locates this family still in Justice Precinct #2. Red River County, TX. There were five children in the family at that time; Myrtle Lee; John T.; Ethel; Cecil A. and Cora W. Grover Speir was then missing from the family unit.

The 1940 Texas, Red River County listed the family living in Bogata on Avenue A. There was William B., a Blacksmith, Cora E. his wife and their daughter Myrtle who was noted as an (telephone) operator. The family's last name on this census was written as Spears. One line listed just before this family's listing was the family of Julius L. King who happened to be Speir's son-in-law married to his daughter Willie (Cora) S. King and their three children.

William stayed active in his business for the next fifty-two years until he was forced into retirement by a stroke at the age of 75 in 1947. He was a Mason operating a blacksmith shop and grist mill at the approximate location of the First National Bank in Bogata. Although his stuttering made it difficult for casual acquaintances to follow his speech, he possessed a keen intellect holding a patent for the suspension system for the Model T Ford. He survived the amputation of a leg at age 85, living to the age of 92 under the care of his daughter Myrtle.

Cora Tucker Speir died on July 19, 1946. William Baker Speir died at a Bogata Nursing Home on May 31, 1964. An obituary for Mr. Speir was found in the newspaper *The Paris News*, Paris, TX, dated Monday, June 1, 1964. Services were held at the Bogata Methodist Church, Masonic Rites were performed at the cemetery with Masons serving as pallbearers.

Cora and William Speir are both buried at Smith Cemetery near Rosalie. They were the parents of seven known children.

1. Grover Levoy Speir
2. Mary Myrtle Leota Speir
3. John Thomas Speir
4. Ethel Speir
5. Effie Speir, born Nov. 7, 1900, twin to Ethel, died 1900
6. Cecil Andrew (Jack) Speir
7. Cora Willie Speir

Grover Levoy Speir

Grover L. Speir was born January 17, 1893, in Cove, Polk County, Arkansas the son of William Baker Speir and Cora Etta Lee Tucker. Grover moved with his family to the Indian Territory in the late 1900s, then into Red River County, Texas where he was found enumerated with his family for the 1900 census. Grover grew up working in the blacksmith shop of his father and as the other Speir boys came along the shop was turned into a business as Mr. Speir did the blacksmithing Grover did the horseshoeing and the two other boys John and Jack shared the mechanic business. Mr. Speir showed Grover how to set his first shoe when he was eleven years old.

Grover served for four years with the U. S. Cavalry during the Franciscon (Poncho) Villa uprising. He enlisted at Shawnee, OK, after riding and walking from his Texas home, eventually reporting for duty at Fort Logden, CO. He spent a 4-year hitch with the Cavalry rose to the rank of Sgt. working as a furrier in 'C' Troop, 3rd Cavalry. He also worked as an armorer with expertise in the Gatling gun.

A story passed down through the Speir family alleges Villa's agents kidnapped Grover forcing him to work training Villa's armorers and gunners. He rode with Villa's army for several months. After he learned he was about to be shot, he escaped making his way back to Ft. Bliss in El Pasco.

Grover married Willie Mae Westbrook the daughter of James Thomas Westbrook and Ollie Kate Thompson and the granddaughter of Mr. and Mrs. J. E. Westbrook and Mr. and Mrs. John Thompson. She was born October 3, 1909.

The Grover Speir family was found for the 1940 Texas, Lamar County census where Grover was listed as a proprietor- blacksmith. The census stated he had been living in Rural, Red River, Texas since 1935. There were two children in the family at that time, Martha and Evanda.

Grover worked for over 65 years as a blacksmith and 'horseshoer' most of the time in Bogata, Red River County. He was a colorful and fiercely independent individual. He wore his hair and beard long before it became fashionable, and he drove a horse drawn surrey as his sole means of transportation instead of an automobile. His great niece Debra Carter McCloud remembers meeting him once years ago, at that time his beard extended down to his waist.

An article appeared in the September 24, 1957, issue of the "*Paris News-Weekly Farm New*" entitled "Bogata Blacksmith Spears Recalls Hitch in Cavalry." The article called Grover a "special character around town," who had not locked the doors to his shop in 12 years, in fact there were no doors to the shop. About his long beard, he said he found a clean shave a source of irritation, "Fire from a hot forge will chap the skin...The beard was more of a joke, sort of like fireman wearing red suspenders." The article misspelled his last name, but people of this family are used to that.

Grover died at McCuistion Hospital in East Deport on August 25, 1968, of a myocardial infarction. He was buried at the Highland Cemetery in Deport, TX. Willie Grover died March 18, 2004, she was also buried in Highland Cemetery, Deport, TX. Grover and his wife Willie were the parents of seven known children.

1. Martha Jan Speir
2. Evanda Mae Speir, died as a child
3. Samuel Levoy Speir, 'Sam'
4. Mary Lou Speir
5. Charles Wayne Speir, 'Charlie'
6. James Don Speir, 'Jimmy'
7. William Andrew Speir, 'Andy'

Mary Myrtle Speir

Mary Myrtle Leola Speir was born in the Indian Territory (Oklahoma) in a sod dugout on November 18, 1894, the daughter of William Baker Speir and Cora Etta Lee Tucker Speir. Mary, known as Myrtle, was the telephone operator when phone service was brought to Bogata. She worked the exchange out of her home. She could be called most any time day or night as she slept on a bed in the office. She retired from her manual switchboard after 35 years on the job.

Myrtle's father lived with her during his final days until his death in May 1964. Mary Myrtle Speir died at Red River County Hospital at Clarksville on November 15, 1965, she was 70 years old. The informant for the death certificate was Mary Myrtle's sister Mrs. Ethel Nixon. She was buried at Smith Cemetery in Bogata two days later.

John Thomas Speir

John Thomas Speir was born in Rosalie, Texas on March 15, 1898, the son of William Baker Speir and Cora Etta Lee Tucker. John signed for the World War I Draft Registration on September 12, 1918. His occupation at that time was garage mechanic; his father's name was William B. Speir. John was 5'8" tall, had blue eyes and dark hair.

John married Rose Melvina Parker in 1920. She was born in Arkansas on December 25, 1896, the daughter of William R. Parker and Nancy Penn Parker. She was with her family for the 1900 Texas census living in Justice Precinct #2, Hopkins County.

Rose Parker, Nancy Margaret and John Thomas Speir circa 1935

The 1930 Texas census, Red River County finds the family in Precinct #2. John was working as a mechanic. He worked as a mechanic for several years in Bogata, after which he moved to Paducah, Cottle County, Texas where he was engaged in cotton farming.

John Thomas Speir died of a myocardial infarction on October 31, 1952, at Richards Memorial hospital, in the town of Paducah, Cottle County, Texas. He had been living at Paducah for the past 7 years where he worked as a cotton farmer. Informant for the death certificate was Mrs. J. T. Speir. He was buried at the Bogata Cemetery with the Norris Funeral Home officiating.

Following her husband's death Rose went to live with her son William (Bill) Warren Speir in Childress, Texas. She lived alone for many years until she was well into her 90's. Her last address on the Social Security records was 75417 Bogata, Red River, Texas. Rose died in a rest home in Childress on August 6, 1997, she was buried at Smith Rosalie Cemetery, Rosalie, Red River County Texas.

John T. and Rose Parker Speir were the parents of three known children:

1. Nancy Margaret Speir, married Sherwood J. Carter, see page 46.
2. William Warren Speir, born July 22, 1931 and died on December 11, 2016
3. Jo Ann Speir, born October 19, 1934

Ethel Speir

Ethel Speir was born in Rosalie on November 7, 1900, the daughter of William B. Speir and Cora Etta Lee Tucker. Ethel was a twin to Effie Speir who did not survive. Ethel married Raymond David Nixon of Deport, TX.

Raymond David Nixon was born February 13, 1900, in Lamar County, TX the son of James Battle Nixon and Martha Jane Nixon

The 1940 Texas census, Lamar County shows this family. Raymond was a farmer, there was one child in the family 4 year old Gary L. This family listing was one household above that of Ethel's brother Grover L. Speir.

Ethel Speir Nixon died of respiratory arrest at the McCuistion Hospital on November 30, 1978, in Paris, TX. The informant for the death certificate was her son James B. Nixon. She was buried in the Highland Cemetery, Deport, TX. Raymond died October 13, 1985, at Paris, Lamar County, TX. He was buried alongside his wife Ethel in the Highland Cemetery, Deport, TX.

Ethel and Raymond Nixon were the parents of three known children.

1. Raymond Levoy Nixon, died as an infant
2. Gary Lane Nixon
3. James Baker Nixon

Cecil Andrew Speir

Cecil Andrew Speir was born in Rosalie, Texas on June 22, 1904, the son of William Baker Speir and Cora Etta Lee Tucker. Cecil, better known as Jack, worker as an automobile mechanic in Bogata. He married Pearl Johnson of Lamar County some time about 1928. She was born in Bolivar Mars, TN on June 10, 1906, the daughter of Jacob M. Johnson and Dora J. Watson.

This young family was found on the Oklahoma 1930 census, Brown Township, Seminole County. Their only child, Jackie Jr. was 6/12-year-old born in Texas which means the family had just recently moved to Oklahoma. Jack was a mechanic working in a repair shop.

The family was found for the 1940 Texas census living in Paris, Lamar County, Texas. There were two children in the home at that time Jackie Speir, age 10 and Seredish, age 9. Jack's occupation was given as Oil Field Worker in an industry call 'Ruffneck'.

The family moved to Shawnee, OK, in 1943, where Jack established a successful mechanic business, later investing in oil and gas leases becoming successful in that venture. He owned and operated the Park Street garage.

Cecil A. "Jack" Speir of 638 West Dewey died Friday evening in a local hospital on May 24, 1957, in Shawnee, Pottawatomie, OK. He had suffered a heart attack about two weeks before his death. He was buried in Resthaven Memorial Park, Shawnee, OK. Jack was survived by his wife Pearl, two daughters, Mrs. Jackie Wood, 1212 East 11th and Mrs. Serita Fox, Ponce City, one granddaughter Morena Wood and two grandsons, Gerald Wood and Kevin Fox.

Jack was also survived by his father W. B. Speir, of Bogata; one brother G. L. Speir of Bogata; three sisters Miss Myrtle Speir of Bogata, Mrs. Ethel Nixon and Mrs. Willie (Cora) King, both of Lubbock, TX. Funeral services were held in the Roesch Brothers Chapel, the Rev. George L. Needham, pastor of Wesley Methodist Church, officiating. Obituary found in *Shawnee News-Star, Sunday May 26, 1957.*

Pearl Johnson Speir died on January 24, 1997; she too was buried in Resthaven Memorial Park. Her address at the time of her death was 74145 Tulsa, Tulsa, OK.

There were two known children of this marriage:

1. Jackie Speir
2. Serita Speir

Cora Willie Speir

Cora Willie Speir was born in Rosalie, Red River County, TX, on March 2, 1910, the daughter of William Baker Speir and Cora Etta Lee Tucker. Cora married Julius Lafayette King of Bogata in Hugo, OK in February 1930. Julius, better known as 'Tobe' was a farmer born about 1910, the son of William Walter King and Martha Anglin Baty.

This young family was found on the 1940 Texas census Red River County living in Bogata. Julius was working as a road oiler in the road improvement industry. There were three children at that time, Fayette King, age 9, Gerald King, age 7 and Patricia King age 2. The King family was living one door from Cora's Speir family.

On March 6, 1972, Julius had an amendment to his birth certificate recorded by the state. When he was born the first name part of his birth certificate was left blank. On the affidavit of Lee King dated March 2, 1972, the blanks on his certificate were filled in recording his name and the names of his parents.

Julius Lafayette King died November 29, 1987; he was buried in Bogata Cemetery. Cora Speir King died on December 12, 1994; she was buried in the Bogata Cemetery. They share one stone with both of their names on it.

There were six known children of this marriage.

1. Julius Fayette King

2. Gerald Lee King
3. Patricia Ann King
4. Lynna June King
5. Cheryl Elaine King
6. Karen Elizabeth King

Belle Speir

Belle Speir was born on September 15, 1888, the daughter of Francis M. Speir and Mary Lane. Belle Speir married T. C. (Thomas Clinton) Cheatwood on October 23, 1894, in Polk County, Arkansas. He was the son of Charles Jordon Cheatwood and Kathryn Julia Daniels. Both of the young people were from the town of Cove, he was 19 years old, she was 17. Belle's mother Mary Speir in a note given to the clerk gave her permission for the wedding.

The young couple were found on the 1900 census living in the Chickasaw Nations, Indian Territory. There one child in the home, Charles M. Cheatwood, age 2. The 1910 Oklahoma census Elmore, Garvin, OK; there was one child in the home, Charls Cheatwood, age 12 and Belle's mother, Marry(sic) Spire(sic).

Clinton Cheatwood registered for the draft on September 2, 1918, in McClain County, Purcell, OK. His date of birth was given as October 30, 1873, he was described as 5'6" tall with blue eye and brown eyes. The 1930 Texas, Collingsworth County census locates this family, there were no children in the home at that time. The 1840 Texas census in same county finds the same situation, no children recorded.

Thomas Clinton Cheatwood died on July 22, 1962, at his home which was noted as "14 miles S. W. of Shamrock" in Collingsworth County, TX. His occupation was listed as farmer with an industry of "Row Crops." He was buried in Dozier Cemetery, Dozier, TX. Informant was his wife Mrs. Effie Cheatwood. Belle over time had become Effie Cheatwood, she died April 24, 1980. A death certificate for her has not yet been found. She outlived all her children. She and her husband share a headstone in Dozier Cemetery, Dozier, TX.

The Find A Grave Memorial Web site list 7 siblings for Thomas Clinton Cheatwood but no children.

Thomas Jefferson Speir

Thomas Jefferson Speir was born in Gainesville, Cooke County, TX on April 5, 1879, the son of Francis M. Speir and Mary Lane. Frequently known as Jeff, he married Ella _____.

The 1910 Oklahoma, Paden, Okfuskee County census locates the Thomas J. Speir family. He was a farmer 31 years old, while his wife Ella was 21 years old. There was a 4-year-old child named Loyd T. Speir in the family and a one year old child named Gracie Ralston.

The 1920 Oklahoma census, Paden, Okfuskee County shows T. J. Speir a widower with five children, Loyd Speir, age 14, Millie Speir, age 9, Mable Speir, age 6, Hubert Speir, age 4, and Norma Speir, age 2 and Gracie Ralston, age 11.

The 1930 Texas census, Donley County, shows this family, there were three children in the family at this time, Loyd T. Speir, age 24, Hubert A. Speir, age 15, and Norma J. Speir

Jeff was living in household of his brother James Y. Speir for the 1940 Texas, Hidalgo County census.

Thomas J. Speir died on December 13, 1954, of carcinoma of the stomach. The informant on the death certificate was Lloyd Speir. Thomas was buried in Weslaco Cemetery, Weslaco, TX.

John Clayton Speir

John Clayton Speir was born in Indian Territory (Oklahoma) on August 26, 1881, the son of Francis M. Speir and Mary Lane.

John C. Speir, age 82, died of bronchopneumonia due to a fracture of the femur at the Memorial Old folks home, Waslaco, Hidalgo County, TX on August 4, 1964. His daughter Opal Wright signed the death certificate. He was buried in Roselawn Cemetery, McAllen, TX.

James Yancy Speir

James Yancy Speir was born April 9, 1884, in Cove, Polk County, Arkansas, the son of Frances M. Speir and Mary Lane (information taken from a February 1937 Social Security application). James, known by friends and family as 'Yank,' married Florence Knowles on ___. She was born in Cookeville, Titus County, TX on March 20, 1889, the daughter of John Franklin Knowles and Elizabeth Putman.

James Y. Speir family was found on the 1920 Texas census living in Justice Precinct 3, Lamar County. His wife's name was Florence Speir with four children listed, Alvin Speir, age 13, Susie Speir, age 11, Lucille Speir, age 8 and Frances Speir, age 2. James was a farmer.

For the 1930 census the family was living in Donley County, TX. The children at that listing were Alvin, Lucille, Francis(son), R. L.(son) and Virginia. The 1940 Texas, Hidalgo County census lists the following children, Robert L., Virginia D. and Gilda R. James's 61-year-old brother Jeff Speir was the last entry for the family.

James Yancy Speir died on July 1, 1949, at the McAllen Municipal Hospital, McAllen, Texas, Hidalgo County. He was a retired farmer. The informant was James F. Speir. Mr. Speir was buried at Rose Lawn with the Kreidler-Pride Funeral home officiating. Florence Knowles Speir died November 11, 1972, at the McAllen General Hospital. The informant for the certificate was her daughter Mrs. Fred Rock. She was buried in Roselawn Cemetery, McAllen, TX, with funeral director H. M. Kreidler officiating. James and Florence have separate stones but are side-by-side.

There were seven known children of this family.

1. Alvin Speir
2. Susie Speir

3. Lucille Speir
4. Frances Speir
5. Robert L. Speir
6. Virginia D. Speir
7. Gilda R. Speir

George Carroll Speir

George Carroll Speir was born on October 6, 1886, in Cove, Polk County, Arkansas, the son of Francis M. Speir and Mary Lane. George, known to his family and friends as 'Cad,' married Mollie Hatfield of Wise County, TX.

The 1930 census, Precinct #1 Donley County, TX locates this family, there were six children within the home at this listing. He was a farmer working on his own account.

George C. Speir died December 23, 1972, in the nursing center at the Palo Pinto General Hospital. The hospital is located in the town of Mineral Wells, Palo Pinto County, Texas. He was buried in Woodland Park Cemetery, Mineral Wells, TX.

There were six known children of this family.

1. Ethel Speir, age 18, 1930 census
2. Casper Speir, age 17, 1930 census
3. Millard Speir, age 12, 1930 census
4. Helen Speir, age 9, 1930 census
5. Carrol Speir, age 6, 1930 census
6. Charles Speir, age 3 and 8/12, 1930 census

THE PARKER FAMILY

William Riley Parker

William Riley Parker was born in Alabama in September 1856, the son of William C. Parker and Lucinda Borden. William married Nancy Jane Penn about the year 1877, time and place unknown. Nancy was born August 25, 1858, in Alabama the daughter of William Parish Penn and Phoebe Caroline Barnett Penn. The young couple was found on the 1880 Alabama census living in Lawrence County, Township 8 Range 8. William was listed as Riley Parker, a farmer and Nancy, "keeping house" with one child William age 3.

The William R. Parker family was located on the 1900 Texas census living in Hopkins County, Justice Precinct No. 2. He was a farmer, the family recorded that there were 7 children out of 10 still living. The family rented the property where they were living. All the children except the last were born in Alabama, he was born in Texas.

The 1910 Texas census, Morris County locates the family. William was working as a Blacksmith owning his own shop. There were only four children in the home at this listing, Carrie B., Rose M, William M. and Alee? The 1920 Texas census locates the family in Red River County, Justice Precinct #2. There were two children in the family, Rose M., age 22 and Alee?, age 16.

The 1930 Texas census, Red River County locates William R. and Nancy J. Parker living in Justice Precinct # 2. The 73-year-old William R. Parker was still working as a Blacksmith. There were no children listed for the family. However, eight listings further down the page finds the family of John T. Speir, his wife Rose M. Speir and their 7-year-old daughter Nancy M. Speir. Both families were living along the Rosalie & Johntown Road.

Nancy Jane Parker age 77 years died June 18, 1935, at Bogata, Red River County, Texas. She was buried in the Smith-Rosalie Cemetery. The informant for the death certificate was her husband W. R. Parker.

William R. Parker died in 1945. He was buried at Fairmount Cemetery, Hollis, Harmon County, OK, age 90 years. There is a slightly bruised masonry stone at the cemetery that has the name WR Parker in raised letters and below the name the dates 1855 and 1945. This information was found on the Internet under the site *Find A Grave Memorial.* This site also listed his spouse as Nancy Jane Parker and four children, Lucinda E. Parker Homer (1882-1957), George Wellis Parker (1889-1960), Sarah Caroline Parker Barnett (1895-1918) and Rose Melvina Parker Speir (1896-1997).

The children of William R. and Nancy Penn Parker:

1. William Parker, born about 1877
2. Lucinda E. Parker, born in May 1883
3. Jas M. Parker, born Jan. 1886
4. Geo. W. Parker, born July 1888
5. Sarah Caroline Parker, born June 1894 (nickname probably Carrie)
6. Rose M. Parker, born Dec. 1896

7. Wm. M. Parker, born 1900
8. Ince? L. Parker, born 1904 (Alee)?

Index

Index

Index

Index

Index